Glenna is an excellent
God dwelling with his
she weaves in her personal stories of pain and loss in memoir
fashion, we journey with her on a discovery of new and more
meaningful ways that God is always near and good and faithful
and kind and enough. Overall, I was convicted in the sweetest
way to remember that abiding in the Lord's presence through
his Word is enough for me in the midst of my every fear, unmet
desire, struggle, and joy.

—**Kristie Anyabwile**, Editor, *His Testimonies, My Heritage*

Glenna Marshall has done it. In her book, *The Promise Is His
Presence*, she has managed to pull off a balance that is rare among
Christian authors: a book that clearly and accurately portrays
the story of redemption reflected throughout the Bible while
also connecting it with the author's very gripping, heartbreak-
ing, and inspiring personal story of suffering. With her beautiful
writing style, she reminds us that the answer to joy in suffering
is not the alleviation of suffering but the reality of God's presence in it. I commend this book to all those who are seeking
the secret to experiencing the nearness of God in the darkest
of places.

—**Brian Croft**, Senior Pastor, Auburndale Baptist Church,
Louisville, Kentucky; Founder, Practical Shepherding

If you are weary, discouraged, or suffering, you will find refresh-
ment, encouragement, and comfort in these pages. Glenna Marshall masterfully combines biblical truth and relatable personal
narrative to explore the doctrine of God's presence with his people. The result is a stunning display of the hope, joy, and peace
that we have because of God's presence with us.

—**Marissa Henley**, Author, *Loving Your Friend through Can-
cer: Moving beyond "I'm Sorry" to Meaningful Support*

I resonate deeply with the title and message of this book. The promise of God's presence has sustained me through the darkest days of my life and has given me hope for the future. This is Glenna's story, too, and she writes of the pain we all face—not with pithy clichés but rather with deep, experiential knowledge. She gives voice to our humanity while consistently pointing us to the goodness of God. I am thankful.

—**Christine Hoover**, Author, *Searching for Spring: How God Makes All Things Beautiful in Time* and *Messy Beautiful Friendship: Finding and Nurturing Deep and Lasting Relationships*

In *The Promise Is His Presence*, Glenna Marshall repeatedly speaks a beautiful truth—that in our painful struggle, though we may never find out the *why* behind our sorrows or see *how* we will make it through them, because of Immanuel we know *who* dwells with us in our suffering. Marshall reminds us again and again that the most important thing for us to remember is *who*—in our wanderings, God has given us himself, and that is the greatest promise he could ever keep.

—**Abby Ross Hutto**, Author, *God for Us: Discovering the Heart of the Father through the Life of the Son*

In this book that is achingly beautiful and brimming with gospel truth, Glenna Marshall follows the thread of God's goodness and faithfulness throughout the entirety of Scripture while also seamlessly weaving in her own path of pain and suffering. This is a charge to God's people to remember that the point of our trials isn't how quickly we can barrel through them but, rather, who we can come to know and love more deeply along the way. I found a fellow sojourner and was reminded of a faithful shepherd in *The Promise Is His Presence*.

—**Gillian Marchenko**, Author, *Still Life: A Memoir of Living Fully with Depression*

A truly refreshing read that has forever changed my perspective on suffering. Where is God when we suffer? Glenna Marshall's personal journey of suffering reminds us that the problem is not that God is not present but that we look for evidence of his presence in the wrong places. Whether you are walking through the valley of broken dreams or stuck in a rut of spiritual dryness, Marshall shows us just how God's presence can answer every longing of our hearts.

—**Sara Wallace**, Author, *For the Love of Discipline: When the Gospel Meets Tantrums and Time-Outs* and *Created to Care: God's Truth for Anxious Moms*

Do *you* have any thoughts on this book?
Consider writing a review online.
The author appreciates your feedback!

Or write to P&R at editorial@prpbooks.com with your comments. We'd love to hear from you.

# *the promise is* His Presence

WHY GOD IS ALWAYS ENOUGH

glenna marshall

**P&R**
PUBLISHING
P.O. BOX 817 • PHILLIPSBURG • NEW JERSEY 08865-0817

**Library of Congress Cataloging-in-Publication Data**

Names: Marshall, Glenna, author.
Title: The promise is his presence : why God is always enough / Glenna Marshall.
Description: Phillipsburg : P&R Publishing, 2019.
Identifiers: LCCN 2019005644| ISBN 9781629954738 (pbk.) | ISBN 9781629954745 (epub) | ISBN 9781629954752 (mobi)
Subjects: LCSH: God (Christianity)--Omnipresence. | Spirituality--Christianity. | God (Christianity)--Omnipresence--Biblical teaching.
Classification: LCC BT132 .M37 2019 | DDC 231.7--dc23
LC record available at https://lccn.loc.gov/2019005644

To William,
my companion on this tangle of dark and beautiful roads.
The grip of your faithful hand brightens every
shared sorrow and multiplies every joy.

*But as for me, God's presence is my good.*
*I have made the Lord GOD my refuge,*
*so I can tell about all You do.*

—PSALM 73:28

# Contents

# Acknowledgments

I like to think of writing as a solitary activity. And mostly that's true. I've never birthed a baby—a fact you'll see soon enough, in the following pages—but I imagine that the anticipation I've felt while laboring to write the words of this book has been a tiny bit like waiting for a child to arrive. While birth is largely a solitary effort, there are usually a lot of helpful people involved who make the experience as smooth as possible. I'd like to thank the people in my life who helped me birth this book.

Thank you to Amanda Martin and Kristi James of P&R Publishing for helping me say what I want to say in the best way possible. I'm so grateful for your work as editors. Amanda, your patience and careful edits have helped me to become a better writer. Kristi, you helped me to step back and see the bigger picture when I felt overwhelmed by the task before me. Thank you to my writer friend, Marissa Henley, for believing that these words should be read and for putting action and hard work behind that belief. Your generosity and cheerleading have been sweet encouragements to me. Thank you for answering a thousand frantic Voxer messages.

To the people of Trinity Baptist Church: in your presence the Lord has broken my heart and healed it. You are the means by which He has healed me. Thank you for standing by us all those broken years and for standing by us still. You are one of God's sweetest gifts to me, and I love you deeply.

Deepest thanks to Beth, Ranelle, Sue, and Dora for holding me accountable and making sure I am looking at life through the lens of the gospel. Thank you for praying me through this book. To my Thursday afternoon Bible study ladies: you are regularly a breath of fresh air. You always asked about the book, prayed for me as I wrote it, and challenged me to search the Scriptures deeply. But mostly you let me sit with a cup of coffee and a notebook as a fellow participant—and nothing more. Not writer or pastor's wife or teacher. Just me. How I needed those hours with you.

Thank you to Larry, Theda, and Colby Williams of Parengo Coffee in Sikeston, Missouri. You supplied me with endless cups of coffee, a regularly open table, and consistent encouragement to meet my word-count goals when I wrote in your shop. Andrew Peterson, your music got me through all of the Old Testament material and prodded me to look deeper into its stories for the real people beneath the words.

Mom and Dad, thank you for buying me that first journal when I was seven. I remember the empty pages that were begging to be filled with words. Thirty years later, I'm still pouring out all that the Lord teaches me onto every blank page I can find. Thank you for sharing in my joy and for teaching me about Jesus in the very first place. To my sister, Lauren: your pep talks about doing the thing that I love *no matter what* urged me to open that very first blank document on my laptop. It has been a treasure to speak freely about using our gifts for the Lord.

Isaiah and Ian, you are two of God's sweetest expressions of grace to me. When life seemed too broken for hope, the Lord gave you to me and made this barren woman a joyous mother. I will never have enough good words for what you mean to me.

William, you know every page firsthand. I'm sorry for all the ledge-counseling you had to do, but I knew this would be a team effort. You make everything I do better. Thank you for giving me your days off so I could write. Thank you for talking me through the very first seeds of this book and for helping me to believe that it needed to be written down. I would never—could never—have done this without your encouragement. When I am afraid, you gently push me to be the woman God has made me to be.

Jesus, You are everything. I have doubted more than I believed, but You have been with me everywhere I have gone. Thank You for breaking down my life with pain and sorrow so that You could bind me up with Your goodness. I would never have known how much I needed You.

.

# Introduction

# Like a Recurring Dream

*Having the reality of God's presence is not dependent on our being in a particular circumstance or place, but is only dependent on our determination to keep the Lord before us continually.*

—OSWALD CHAMBERS

I have a recurring dream that I'm eight years old, gap-toothed, and wandering my childhood church. My ponytail bounces as I run up and down stairs, searching for something. *Something.* I'm not sure what. I pass classrooms lit with fluorescent bulbs and flashes of memory. Down the darkened stairway connecting the choir loft with the basement, which still smells of old hymnals and polyester robes, I look in all the right places and even in the ones that I suspect will turn up nothing.

I've never found it—nor do I even know what *it* is. Whenever I have that dream, I'm forever stuck in a loop of roaming but never landing on what it is that I'm looking for—I'm only certain that I'll know when I've found it.

The presence of God feels like that, doesn't it? We're not sure exactly how to describe or locate it, but we're certain we'll know when we experience it. It seems like an elusive dream that we try to manufacture in our church services with low lighting, soft music, and persuasive sermons that pull at emotional heart-strings. The modern-day American church strives to create an atmosphere that convinces us that God is with us.

But what if I told you that no stage-setting is necessary? That the presence of God is not something we can reproduce or manipulate with the right guitar chord or turn of phrase but rather something we can enjoy at all times? God has promised us the gift of His presence, all throughout Scripture. And it's a promise that He continues to keep today. We don't have to go looking for it, we don't have to attempt to manufacture it and package it for redistribution, and we don't have to wonder if we'll ever find it. Those of us who have believed in Christ Jesus for the atonement of our sins already have everything we're looking for.

## Awakening to God's Presence

It wasn't until I was in my early thirties that I realized that God's presence was the answer to all my heart's longings and desires. God used a decade of suffering in order to pull back the veil and show me how my trials—which included infertility, chronic illness, and profound church hurt—were avenues for me to understand the importance and magnitude of His nearness.

It happened slowly, like the long-awaited greening of the trees after a brutal winter. The branches are empty and dark against a bleak, gray sky, but one day there's the barest of green—a whisper, really—on the trees. The sky warms, and then one morning you're driving down the street and it hits you that the world has turned flowery and brushed with green again. When did it happen? Incrementally—but you didn't see the process. You only remember the before, maybe the middle, and the after.

My awakening to God's presence began during a bleak winter, both physically and spiritually. I was convinced that God didn't much like me. I knew Scripture was my only place to go for help;

I'd tried everything else. I didn't know exactly what I was looking for—hope, maybe. Or something that I knew I wouldn't find: a promise that the Lord would change my circumstances. But I'd exhausted every other resource. So I kept reading, searching for the secret answer to my troubles but feeling that the search was time poorly spent.

One day, I opened a new journal and penned an entry. The next morning, I reread it and realized I had merely cataloged all the ways that God had abandoned me . . . just as I had in every journal entry for the previous six months. Something had to change. I kept looking for *me* in my Bible, but all I found were words that I couldn't connect to my life.

In desperation, I switched tactics. I bought a stack of spiral notebooks. I began in the book of Isaiah and scribbled down every phrase about God, every character trait, every random thought about His personhood that struck me as I read. A few months later, a hint of green appeared on the trees outside, and I realized that the Bible was bursting with one truth that I needed more than anything else: God was with me.

### The Wonder Years

I had a nine-month jump on church attendance before I was even born. Both of my parents were raised in church, and their first-generation believer parents passed down a heritage of faith that I am privileged to call my own. I was taught the gospel from infancy, and it wasn't hard for my young heart to believe I was a sinner in need of a Savior.

At the age of six, I completed my first Bible drill (that Scripture-memorization competition that was well known in conservative churches during the late 1980s). Not only could I recite all the books of the Bible, I also knew many of the bricks in the "Roman road." I understood that I could either pay for my sins in hell or believe that Jesus paid for them at the cross. Even at a tender age, I could see that I had to do something with Jesus. He couldn't just hang on the felt cross on the flannel board of my elementary Sunday school class. I had to decide whether He was what I wanted my life to be about. Grasping as much as a six-year-old can, I professed faith in Christ and was baptized.

Faith was easy when I was a child. My mom tells stories about finding crumpled notes in my pockets while she would sort laundry to be washed. She'd smooth out the papers to find love letters written to Jesus in my crooked handwriting. I believed that He was as close as air, and I sang made-up songs to Him while swinging on the swing set in our backyard. Part triune Creator, part invisible friend—there was no reason to doubt that God loved me and was always with me. I belonged to Him, and He belonged to me.

Growing up in a two-parent Christian home in the sequestered Bible Belt of the South, I ran into little that one could call "suffering." I had no notions of what the word even meant beyond the fear of losing a parent or the threat of the notorious springtime tornadoes that we experienced from year to year. The greatest trouble I faced was wondering whether my old, unreliable car would start in the morning or would spend another day broken down in our driveway.

Suffering was something that happened to other people. But we were *blessed*. We were different because we loved Jesus. And I thought that was enough to keep us safe from suffering. But it wasn't. What I didn't understand until decades later is that following Jesus doesn't protect you from suffering. Sometimes, following Jesus is the very path into it.

When you look at your life, your trials, unfulfilled longings, and sorrows may tell you a story of absence. Suffering may seem like a note telling you that God has left you to handle things yourself. "You're on your own. Be back soon." But when we look at the story of Scripture we see that suffering is often the letter, the envelope, the emissary that bears a different message. Suffering may be the way God makes certain that you know the truth: *He is with you.*

## God's Presence in History

Throughout the Old Testament, one of the most notable characteristics that set God apart from the pagan gods of other nations was His presence among His people. God spoke to His people directly, and He communicated through judges, prophets, and priests. He showed up in flames of fire and columns of clouds to guide His people to the land He had promised to give them. He even designated a location for His presence to dwell—the tabernacle and, later, the temple—so that His people would *know* without a doubt that He was with them.

He was different from the gods of the other nations because He was steadfast, unchanging, reliable. His presence made the people victorious in battle and drove them to their knees in reverent fear. His presence was an unmistakable demonstration of His power and holiness.

But what about today? We don't come away from prayer time with a glowing face like Moses. Though I live on a major seismic fault line, I haven't felt the earth tremble during my Bible study, and I've never been warned not to touch a mountain for fear of falling dead.

No, the presence of God in my life two thousand years after Christ has been more like the still, small voice heard by the prophet Elijah and less like the blaze of a fire or the fearsome force of a whirlwind. One major difference between Elijah's encounter with God's presence and ours, however, is that the voice he heard was audible and caused him to cover his face in fear, while the voice that we hear is wrapped in ancient words of the Bible, which remind us that we can approach God boldly, *without* fear.

He's the same God, but history was split in two when Jesus took our sin on Himself at the cross. The way we understand and experience His presence changed.[1] What hasn't changed, though, is that God's presence is meant to be our comfort—and we can trace that thread of surety throughout the history of Israel. The God who appeared in a burning bush and made His presence known in a pillar of cloud and fire, the God who dwelled in the tent in the midst of His people, the God whose glory filled the temple—this very same God is with us! He is still keeping His promise to be with us.

Jesus's incarnation, death, and resurrection ushered in the new covenant, in which the grafted-in members of God's family are afforded the wealth of His presence in our very selves. The dwelling place of God became the heart of every believer in Christ. And until we meet Him face-to-face in heaven, God's presence in our lives is sufficient to propel us through every confusing uncertainty and every painful trial.

My path toward the belief that God's presence is enough was a rocky, winding one. It took me a long time to understand that the promise of Scripture isn't that my life will be free from suffering but rather that I will feel God's nearness in it. Infertility, a floundering ministry, chronic physical pain, family instability—these are some of the things God has used in my life to teach me to trust Him and find satisfaction in His presence.

When I reflect back over my past years of struggle, I hear echoes of Eden, whispers of wilderness, cries of captivity. My longings for soul satisfaction have mirrored those of God's people throughout redemptive history, and, like the Israelites, I have worshiped both God and the things that I thought would make

---

1. God is the same God in all Scripture. His character remains constant throughout all of history. What I'm referring to here is *progressive revelation*. In other words, though the way we understand and have access to Him has changed with the new covenant, God Himself has not changed.

me happy. I've struggled to believe that the knowledge that God is with me could be enough for me to trust Him with my list of unanswered prayers. But what we see from the big story of the Bible is that God has promised His presence over and over to His people. In being with His people, God gave them everything they needed. When they questioned whether He was enough, they turned to worship something else. When *we* question whether He is enough, we turn to worship something else. Rejecting the truth that God's presence is enough for us will always lead us to idolatry. We're not a lot different from the Israelites, really. But we get to see an even fuller picture of God's promise of presence! As we follow the story of our present God throughout the whole Bible, we can see that the answer to what we long for is found in His unchanging, constant presence. His presence with us gives us enough comfort for our sorrows, enough contentment for our deferred hopes, enough patience for our waiting, enough perseverance for our pain. He is enough!

I want to show you that the promise of God's presence is more than a sentiment we offer ourselves when our hearts yearn for what we cannot find. I want to help you see that God uses our longings, this side of heaven, to keep us close to Him until we see Him face-to-face. As we walk through the time line of Scripture, I hope you'll see your place in God's big story. He who has kept His promise of presence throughout all history will keep that promise to you.

# Part 1

## What We Lost in the Garden

# 1

# The Fall and
# Everything After

*There is no time in human history when you were more
perfectly represented than in the Garden of Eden.*

—R.C. Sproul

On a cold February day, I found myself lying on a frigid steel operating table for the third time in seven years. One nurse applied inflatable compression wraps to my calves while another pressed a mask over my face. A stream of pure oxygen brought an odd mix of relaxation and panic to my chest. I had put off this surgery for a while because I didn't want to take the time for recovery. But then one day I couldn't talk through the pain or get up from the floor, and I knew I was out of time.

"Stupid Eve," I've often grumbled. "Why couldn't she have ignored the snake and the fruit and just said, 'No thanks; none for me today'?"

Eve's curse hasn't meant that my anguish in childbirth has increased—although, from what I hear, the pain of delivering a child isn't exactly a walk in the park. I've watched enough episodes of *Call the Midwife* to understand that it takes something beyond normal human strength to birth a child. But I don't know that personally—because for me, Eve's curse has meant anguish over ever having children *at all*. I have endometriosis—a disease that has fused together my abdominal organs, repeatedly gripped me with blinding pain, and left me with nearly no hope of pregnancy. This surgery was another attempt to temporarily treat its effects.

*Third time's the charm*, I thought. I thanked the nurses awkwardly and counted backward from one hundred as medicated sleep crowded out my consciousness.

## What We Lost in the Garden

Eve's curse isn't the beginning of the story. The beginning was actually very good. When God set Adam and Eve in the garden of Eden, His relationship with them was unbroken. The couple enjoyed a fullness of His presence. It's hard for me to wrap my mind around that kind of friendship with God—for that is what they seemed to have: a *friendship*. In the garden, Adam and Eve had all the varieties of food a heart should desire, authority over the animal kingdom, and an up-close, face-to-face relationship with their Creator. They needed nothing more.

So when the deceiver came to Eve and suggested that she eat from the only prohibited tree in the garden, his words were weighted with the allure of more than just a tasty bite of fruit. It wasn't enough for her and Adam to simply be *with* God in Eden; they ought to pursue something *more* than God. Convinced that God was holding out on them, Adam and Eve desired to be *like* Him. In tempting them to reach for more, Satan was actually tempting them to settle for less.

Forfeiting everything that was good for them, our first parents fell headlong into idolatry and self-worship. As their teeth broke the skin of the forbidden fruit, they made a crystal-clear proclamation to God: "You are not enough for us." They had

temptation in flesh

sung the opening line of a song of dissatisfaction that we still sing today—a song that is wrapped in discontent and bent toward pride. The refrain has been sung loud and often by the people of God throughout history, and we still sing it today.

We lost a lot when sin entered the world. Everything broke: health, safety, innocence, peace. But our greatest loss was when that face-to-face relationship with God broke. "Then the man and his wife heard the sound of the LORD God walking in the garden at the time of the evening breeze, and they hid themselves from the LORD God among the trees of the garden" (Gen. 3:8). Nestled in that verse is the moment when it all fell apart: "They hid themselves from the LORD God." Newly awakened to what they had done, knowing what they shouldn't know, feeling what they shouldn't feel . . . they hid from God's presence.

When the Lord called out for the hiding couple after they had sinned, shame was their first response, followed quickly by blame. With the taste of forbidden fruit still on their lips, the first man and woman on earth were forced from their home. Their sin of disbelief had severed that face-to-face friendship. Not until heaven will we have the kind of pre-fall relationship with God that Adam and Eve traded for the passing pleasures of sin.

Dressed in the trappings of consequence, they could no longer stand before the God they had known intimately. They could not conceal their nakedness, and they could not cover their guilt. God would have to do both. In a protective order, He forced them from their home to begin an existence marked by new enemies: sin and death. The repercussions of their sin have reached farther than they could have ever imagined.

## What We Gained in the Garden

What did we gain from the fall? Disease, malfunctioning bodies, infertility, and chronic illness are proof that we live in the fallen version of what God created to be good. But when I think of the damaging effects of sin, shame hovers near the top of the list. Guilt and shame, when harnessed rightly, can lead to real repentance—but for some of us, the lingering whisper of shame is always a breath away, bringing nagging reminders that we have missed the mark of God's holiness.

Shame swallows the hope that we fight to believe in. It steals the confidence we have in Jesus's sacrifice on the cross. When we sing our song of dissatisfaction, shame is the countermelody. We may sing, "You are not enough for me" in discontent and pride, or we may sing it with a bowed head and faltering faith in the sufficiency of the cross.

The fall began with Adam and Eve's proud belief that God was inadequate. Its aftermath unfolded in a shame that wrapped itself around their hearts. It squeezed tightly every time Adam fought with the fields to produce food and when an anguished Eve strained against her own body to deliver the first child on earth. The sweat of his brow, her blood on the ground—both must have felt thick with shame over the sin they could not pay for.

Shame is a tightrope walk that has consequences on either side. Tip too far to either side, and you fall into disbelief in God's sufficiency. A seed of doubt about God's character blossoms in the soil of disbelief and produces the low-hanging fruit of discontent. *Maybe God isn't enough. Maybe I need something more (or less.)* It's what Adam and Eve thought.

The truth is that the moment Adam and Eve chose the fruit, we all needed Jesus. Adam and Eve, you and me, and everyone in between. We all needed Jesus—and, in His kind mercy, God was already sending Jesus. To the serpent, God said, "I will put hostility between you and the woman, and between your seed and her seed. He will strike your head, and you will strike his heel" (Gen. 3:15). This is the first inkling of the gospel—of the way God would fix the problem of broken presence with His own presence

. . . His flesh-and-blood presence. And this promise comes fresh on the heels of the first rebellion.

The plan for a Savior had already been enacted, for it had always been the plan. God's strong, faithful love pushed back against the insidious spread of sin. He was already working out His strategy to reestablish His presence among His people. Even though they have historically bucked against His authority, He has regularly asserted His presence and reminded us of it.

### Everything After

Scripture contains the history of God and His people and of their severed relationship. Always God gives Himself; always the people desire something else. His presence with them will always be enough to meet their needs, and yet they always struggle to believe that it is safe to rely only on Him. Still, through the promise of His presence, He continually lavishes faithful love on a people who half-heartedly follow Him until something seemingly better comes along. God's steadfast love for His people is expressed through His nearness—yet the people don't believe that He will be enough for them. Like their ancestors standing naked next to the tree, they cannot resist the allure of whatever they think will be more tangible and gratifying than the presence of their Creator.

This pattern is ingrained in our lives, too. Our desires well up in our chests, and we feed them with every tangible remedy we can find. Maybe we know that only Christ will suffice, but it's easier to quiet our longings with physical things that bring immediate, quantifiable relief. We may curse the curse, but we're resistant to the remedy. God has always been enough for His people, but we've always been on the lookout for something more—even though seeking satisfaction in anything "more" than God's full presence will unquestionably lead to *less*. In His presence is "fullness of joy," the psalmist writes (Ps. 16:11 ESV). His steadfast love is *satisfying* (see Ps. 90:14; 103:4–5). But we are bound and bent to disbelieve the truth. We think we can find fullness elsewhere.

When Yahweh began to make Himself known to His people, He made certain they knew He was with them. We can trace His persistence through the stories of the patriarchs in Genesis. God began with a man named Abram, whom he made the recipient of His promise—a promise to call a group of people who would belong to Him.

God spoke directly to Abram, changed his name to Abraham, and singled him out to receive a worldwide, history-encompassing promise of blessing: "All the peoples on earth will be blessed through you" (Gen. 12:3). The blessing required obedience, though, and it would cost Abraham the familiarity of his home, his family, and the worship of ancient Babylonian gods. God commanded Abraham to leave kin and country in order to begin a new life in a new land with a God who was utterly new to him—a God who spoke directly to him! This was an entirely new way to live, but Abraham obeyed. Undoubtedly, God's presence with him made it clear that He would keep His word. God was laying a path of faithfulness that we can still look back on today with hope.

It was for Abraham's good, and for our own, that God was with him. In being faithful to Abraham, God was faithful to us—because Jesus was the ultimate fulfillment of the promise that Abraham was given. With each generation that we meet in Genesis—whether they're faithful to Him or not; whether they believe His promises or not—God keeps His covenant . . . for His promise of presence wasn't just about them.

God continued to assert His presence when He reassured Abraham's son Isaac to "not be afraid, for I am with you" (Gen. 26:24). He later promised Isaac's son Jacob at Bethel that He wouldn't leave him until He'd done what He had promised. Though Jacob was a deceitful man who played favorites with his children, God would not allow His plans to be thwarted by the foolishness of man. He was intent on keeping the promises He had made to Jacob's grandfather, Abraham. In so doing, God extended kindness and grace to generations on generations of people—including you and me. When Jacob reflected on his life, he recognized the gift of God's nearness: "He has been with me everywhere I have gone" (Gen. 35:3).

God's presence in the lives of the patriarchs reaches beyond the pages of Genesis to all those who are called the children of God. In choosing Israel, in keeping His promises to Abraham, Isaac, and Jacob, God prepared the way for the ultimate Reconciler He had spoken of in Genesis 3. He was already showing His people that He would stoop low to meet their needs.

## A Lot Like Israel

When I was twenty-four years old, a doctor pummeled my future to its knees. She didn't mean to; she was just the messenger. As she patted me on the shoulder awkwardly, I knew that I would never recover from her words: "It is unlikely that you will ever conceive." Just like that, the future that I had assumed and imagined ended in an explosion of grief. No children. Married two years and with a lifetime ahead of me, I couldn't picture it.

Indeed, for the next decade, shards of my dreams rained down on me, slicing deep when they collided with my barrenness. I questioned the sufficiency of God's presence, His love, His provision. My unfulfilled desire for children dissolved my confidence that He was enough for me in every area of discontent I could dig up. He might be enough for me *if* He answered my prayer. Maybe. But from the moment the doctor pulled back the curtain on a childless future, I pieced together the tune of Eden and reckoned that the Lord was coming up short. He's not enough if there's something else that I want but can't have.

Just one week after my future was emptied of its contents, my pastor husband and I packed up a moving truck and began a new life in a new town, a new state, and a new church full of complete strangers. I tried to leave my new label behind me: *infertile*. But it followed me across the state line. Along with all my worldly possessions, I had also brought with me an empty womb, a bitter heart, and serious doubts about God's faithfulness. Unfamiliar as I was with circumstances that I couldn't fix, I found myself ill-equipped to minister to others in their suffering. Tunnel vision impeded my judgment, and, certain that no one could under-stand, I distanced myself from the new church we had joined. Not knowing that turmoil lay beneath the surface of friendly faces and full church pews, we found our fresh ministry dreams crashing down almost as soon as we darkened the door of our new assign-ment. Bitterness and difficult ministry do not make a good team.

A troubling ministry among strangers was difficult. Infertility felt impossible. I was aching to be filled. With a child, I thought. But the absence of children only revealed that my heart hun-gered for something I couldn't reach myself. We're all yearning for something down deep, and we think we know what will fill that ache. Purpose. Marriage. Children. Love. Security. Posses-sions. Health. Ease. Success. Validation. Insert your longing here. I knew what my own heart was truly hungry for when I held each negative pregnancy test up to the light, desperately searching for a second pink line, and again an hour later when I dug the test out of the trash to study it in case I'd missed something. I knew what would settle my anxiety when my weary husband dragged himself through the back door after a pastoral meeting at which he'd been pounded with public opinion.

A friend told me once about an elderly family member who had made a list—an actual, handwritten list on yellow stenogra-pher's paper—of all the things that had gone wrong in his life and how he was upset with God. He would take it out and show it to people—hopeful, I guess, that someone would commiserate and tell him how he'd been dealt a bad hand.

I remember thinking, *Why on earth would you make that list? What's to be gained from it?* That kind of record-keeping personified bitterness to me. But haven't I done the same thing? Made my list. Memorized it. Showed it to people who dared to think that I was sheltered. Held on to it like it mattered more than anything. I was always hungry, always looking for ways to cross things off that list of losses and unmet desires . . . but taking twisted satisfaction in the fact that I had a list at all. You couldn't dismiss me if I had a list, and I felt dismissed.

I am not unique. Longings and lists and validation—we all know well the trappings of discontent. Call it what you want; discontent goes by many names. We lean toward what we lack until we lack no more. We didn't fall far from that tree in Eden.

Perhaps you have a list. Maybe you've shown it to others, or maybe you've kept a quiet accounting in your heart. I want you to know that the remedy will always be found in knowing the Lord who loves you and is with you. All the way back in Eden, He was making a way to be with His people, and He hasn't changed one bit. He sees your list. He is enough for you, no matter how long your list might be.

## Even in Suffering, Even in Slavery

During the final stretch of the patriarchal period, the book of Genesis makes a sharp turn, steering the narrative down one man's unlikely story. Jacob's son Joseph is known for his timely salvation of Egypt and the surrounding territories when he was put in charge of stockpiling food for an upcoming famine. But before he was known for saving Egypt from starvation, Joseph had a long, painful list of hurts, which started when he was sold into slavery by his own brothers.

But even then, Scripture surprises us by stating that God was *with* Joseph when he was taken to Egypt as a slave. Later, when he was left in prison for years after being accused of aggravated rape, the text reads, "But the LORD was with Joseph and extended kindness to him" (Gen. 39:21).

God extended *kindness* to Joseph through *suffering*. That rubs, doesn't it? Surely that's not kindness! After Joseph was pulled from prison to interpret the Pharaoh's dreams of impending famine, we can glimpse God's goodness in his preserving a generation from starvation. God used Joseph's wisdom to save his own back-stabbing family. But back when he was a forgotten slave in a dark, Egyptian prison, God was with Joseph, and *it was a kindness to him*. God's presence was enough for Joseph to persevere, and this presence was the gift that He kept giving.

Joseph reconciled with his family and moved them to Egypt. Years later, they had multiplied so greatly that the new leadership of Egypt enslaved them in order to control them. They languished as slaves for hundreds of years until God suddenly appeared to a stuttering runaway Hebrew adoptee. When Moses encountered the never-burning, burning bush, God told him to remove his sandals and come no further, for the ground was holy. He commissioned Moses to rescue the Israelites from Egyptian slavery and promised that He would go with Moses. This should have been enough for Moses. The Almighty had appeared in a burning bush that didn't burn up! Yet still Moses voiced his uncertainty. So God pulled out a few signs and miracles to show Moses what He could and would do in front of Pharaoh.

When Moses encouraged the Israelite slaves that God had promised to be their God and to be with them, they didn't listen "because of their broken spirit and hard labor" (Ex. 6:9). Through ten plagues, a reluctant leader with a speech impediment, and a hard-hearted Pharaoh, God delivered His people, brandishing His power as only an omnipotent God can. Why?

I will dwell among the Israelites and be their God. And they will know that I am Yahweh their God, who brought them out of the land of Egypt, *so that I might dwell among them.* I am Yahweh their God. (Ex. 29:45–46)

God delivered Israel so that He could dwell with them, but the idolatry of Egypt was far more familiar to Israel than Yahweh was. The plagues, the wonders, the delivery from such long bondage— God made it clear that this shift meant something. He was their God—and no one, and nothing, else. No little idols of Egypt had delivered them. Not the sun or the moon or any created thing that the Egyptians bowed to. No, Israel now belonged to her Creator. God alone was responsible for the supernatural plagues that had chipped away at Egypt's confidence in retaining the Israelites as slaves. He alone sent the angel to take the breath of every firstborn son in every house that was not marked with the blood of a spotless lamb. The people didn't know about Jesus, but their need for Him throbbed with every opportunity they failed to trust Yahweh.

They obeyed blindly at first. When given freedom, you don't question it. But when the novelty wore off and hardship made its presence known, God's powerful presence didn't seem to be enough for them. Upward floated Eden's familiar refrain: "You are not enough for us." At the precipice of doubt, the people leaned in to their disbelief.

God wasn't surprised. He'd taken them the long way out of Egypt because He knew they'd be tempted to turn back: "The people will change their minds and return to Egypt if they face war," He said (Ex. 13:17). He knew they would bend beneath doubt. To bolster their confidence in His protection, God "went ahead of them in a pillar of cloud to lead them on their way during the day and in a pillar of fire to give them light at night, so that they could travel day or night. The pillar of cloud by day and the pillar of fire by night *never left its place in front of the people*"

31

(Ex. 13:21–22). He set His unmistakable presence in front of the people for twenty-four hours a day in order to guide and protect them. Never did He leave them. Never.

When Pharaoh's army came running after the Israelites, when they were trapped between the sea and the Egyptian army, when they questioned God while He was *in their midst*, He never left them. God opened up the Red Sea and called the people to walk through the middle of it. He pulled the waters apart and led more than a million people through on a dry path. They only had to trust Him and walk. And because it was the only way out, they did. They stood on the other side and watched the Lord conquer their enslavers in one sweeping stroke as He stitched together the waters of the Red Sea. Cloud, fire, rent waters, dead army. God was with them. His presence meant something.

Momentarily, the Israelites seemed to understand who they were following: "When Israel saw the great power that the LORD used against the Egyptians, the people feared the LORD and believed in Him and in His servant Moses" (Ex. 14:31). But their resolve was short-lived. Mere days after the destruction of their enemies, the rumble of hunger in their bellies and the dryness of their throats caused the people to question Yahweh again. Ignoring the cloud and fire, forgetting a split sea and an army of dead Egyptian soldiers, the Israelites grumbled against Yahweh for allowing them to be thirsty.

He provided water, of course, but that didn't mean that they stopped complaining when they felt hungry. "If only we had died by the LORD's hand in the land of Egypt, when we sat by pots of meat and ate all the bread we wanted. Instead, you brought us into this wilderness to make this whole assembly die of hunger!" (Ex. 16:3)

All this complaining and mistrust came quick on the heels of the Red Sea crossing. Their skepticism is impressive! They were hemmed in by the presence of God in fire and clouds.

Yet *my* memory may actually be shorter than theirs. Sitting on a side of the cross that they could never imagine, I struggle to remember the Lord's faithfulness. At the first sign of adversity, I question everything about Him. That first year of negative pregnancy tests began the unraveling of my confidence in Him. The Israelites wanted to be certain that they wouldn't go without food and water. I wanted to be certain that I wouldn't go without children. I would have fit in well among the complaining, grumbling Israelites. I would have led the altos in the song "You are not enough for me."

Like Israel complaining about food when God's presence burned around them, we are foolish to believe that we need God plus something else. You may be tempted to think that if He would just do *this one thing*, then you could be happy in Him. But beneath our desires is one desire that must be met in God. Created to worship Him, we will burn up with misplaced desires if we put anything above Him.

Whatever plagues your heart with longing cannot be answered satisfactorily outside God's faithful presence. He might give you every tangible desire you could ever dream up, but if your heart is not satisfied in Him, you will never stop yearning for more.

We may look at Israel's fragile faith and feel frustration over our own lack of trust, but even in the wreckage of human doubts, the Lord's steadfast nearness shines brightly. Face-to-face with Adam and Eve in the garden, faithfully close to Joseph in his prison, and undoubtedly present at the edges of the Red Sea, He has always been enough.

### Discussion Questions

1. How does the loss of God's face-to-face presence in the garden affect the way that you think about the consequences of sin?

2. Is there an area of your life in which you feel that God is withholding something good from you? How do you fight the temptation to believe that He is not enough for you in that area?

3. Read Romans 8:1–2. Sin severed Adam and Eve's relationship with God, and shame sent them into hiding. How should we as Christians think about shame in light of Jesus's sacrifice on the cross and the presence of the Holy Spirit in us?

4. In Genesis 39, God displayed kindness to Joseph in his suffering. How does the paradox of God's goodness in our suffering help us to persevere? Explain why a biblical approach to suffering might help Christians offer hope to an unbelieving world.

5. If you had witnessed the ten plagues, Israel's exodus from Egypt, the pillar of cloud and of fire, and the parting of the Red Sea, do you think you would have doubted God's faithfulness like the Israelites did? What reasons do you have to trust that God will continue to be faithful to you?

# 2

# Wandering

*From this we may gather that man's nature, so*
*to speak, is a perpetual factory of idols.*

—JOHN CALVIN

In the prequel to the popular children's movie *Despicable Me*, we follow the Minions' search for a master who is bigger than they are. No matter how intimidating their new bosses seem, each one inevitably comes to a fatal end, leaving the Minions to search for another master to follow. It highlights the absurdity of serving a leader who can easily trip and fall off a cliff to his death or be unintentionally murdered by his funny little yellow servants.

The first time I watched *Minions* with my son, I immediately thought of the history of Israel, and then I thought of myself. Our desire to worship someone or something is innate, because we were made to worship God (see Rom. 11:36). Since the fall in Eden, humanity has lived a Minion-like existence of seeking to serve something or someone—with disastrous effects. The Israelites answered their innate need to worship something with the tangible idolatry of Egypt. They worshiped what they knew— what they'd seen worshiped for centuries during their slavery. And while our idolatry doesn't include physical idols, we never seem to have a problem finding something to worship other than the One who made us.

Rather than finding satisfaction in God, we run after masters that can never be what He is, can never love like He does, can never be the holy God deserving of worship. Because we're created to worship Him, nothing else that we want will bring contentment. You can insert whatever desire takes center stage in your head when your alarm goes off in the morning. Whatever you're spending time, money, and relationships to attain—if it's not anchored in God, it won't satisfy the ache in your chest.

### Wounded and Wandering

For me this ache was infertility. For a really long time. My longing reared its head repeatedly and refused to quiet easily. The cycle of cautious hope followed by crashing despair—every single month—took its toll. The wound of infertility reopened regularly, but I was convinced that I could mend it if God wouldn't. I refused to see His hand as anything but withholding. When He didn't give me what I thought I needed, I looked for other ways to fill the ache.

In a voice that was suffused with Israelite wilderness grumbling, I demanded what I thought God should have provided. I didn't think that I was asking too much. I wasn't asking to be famous or wealthy. I was asking for what most people had coming to them, I thought. If God wasn't going to give me any children, well, *I didn't have to be happy about it.* Though it's difficult to admit, I believed that God owed me my own definition of happiness.

When He didn't respond to my anger, I masked it with numbness in order to protect my heart from further pain. Infertility is not the death of one dream; it's the death of many dreams. I went from thinking I'd have a house full of children to daily reabsorbing the reality of zero children. I had to entirely reframe what I thought my future would look like.

If you've faced broken dreams, you get it. You silence your emotions so you won't want what you can't have. Numbness can quickly morph into self-preservation. I frequently found myself stepping away from a circle of chatty moms at church when the conversation turned to morning sickness, childbirth, breastfeeding, stretch marks—all rites of passage for most women, but all foreign and isolating to me. I avoided holding babies and called less often when my friends were pregnant. While my actions weren't *necessarily* sinful, I was miserable while holding people at arm's length. Distancing myself from others may have offered temporary protection, but it did not heal.

Walking wounded, I sloppily bandaged my pain with bitterness and tried to understand why the Lord would not change my circumstances. I thought our relationship was about *how* He would answer my prayers. It never once crossed my mind that *He* was the answer to my prayers. Even while wanting, even while waiting, we can still find contentment in Christ. Or the object of our desires can crowd out everything else. I recognize myself in the Israelites sometimes—demanding to be fed and answered and placated when I already have the One who answers it all.

### Prone to Wander

By the time the people of Israel were free of the Egyptian army, they numbered upward of a million souls (see Ex. 12:37–38). With Moses at the helm and Joshua standing close by, the people needed instruction. They were no longer slaves ruled by a tyrannical Pharaoh, but they didn't know how to live outside of slavery. Before leading them into the land He had promised them, God laid out clear laws on how they were to live as His people.

Though freedom must have seemed attractive, their generations-deep yoke of slavery made it difficult. Belonging to a holy and kind master was foreign to them. They were accustomed to physical idolatry. A living God who intervened rather than standing by in a lifeless piece of stone, who was faithful rather than temperamental, who kept His promises and wanted to be with them—it was all so new! He wanted them to leave behind all that was familiar and to worship Him—an invisible God who couldn't be contained in an idol. Worshiping a God they couldn't see must have been an odd, new beginning.

God made His presence unmistakably clear at Mt. Sinai. Thick smoke, thunder and lightning, and a loud, persistent trumpet sound caused the people to tremble. The ground shook violently, and God's voice was in the thunder. God warned the people not to come near, on pain of death. He was *that* holy. No idol in Egypt could have put on such a display; fear likely kept the people a good, healthy distance from the mountain!

God's holiness prevents sinful man from coming too close, but His goodness makes a way for them to know Him anyway. Though they were sinful, God gave the law as a guideline for how they could enjoy His presence. The laws seem strict but were meant to protect the people and steer them toward holiness. And holiness was likely a completely foreign idea to them! Now that they had been steeped in centuries of empty Egyptian religion, having a relationship with a God who had displayed such power in their deliverance would have been a completely different way of life for them. The people needed to reflect the God whom they served; they needed to be seen as His, not as Egypt's slaves. He was teaching them to be who He had rescued them to be—to wear a new identity that said, "We belong to Yahweh." They needed every instruction in the law so that they wouldn't self-destruct in the empty practices of idol worship.

Even God's discipline was meant to protect and restore them. The pull to worship false gods would always be strong, because every other people group that Israel encountered was steeped in idol worship. The Israelites were the *only* people following

Yahweh. Yet He was clearly the only God worth following—as evidenced by the plagues, the Red Sea, and the pillars of cloud and fire that guarded them.

God appeared in a cloud, and His glory to the Israelites was like a consuming fire. Moses spent forty days receiving the law and the blueprints for the structure where God would dwell among His people. But those very people grew concerned about how long Moses and his helper, Joshua, were taking up on the mountain. In a frenzied panic, they demanded that Moses's brother, Aaron, make an idol for them to worship.

While God made His commitment to Israel clear with plans for a tangible place of residence for His glory, Israel buckled under the pressure of His perceived silence. Aaron made a golden calf out of their donated jewelry and declared a festival to the Lord, fusing his knowledge of Yahweh with the people's desire for a familiar master to worship. In a confusing tangle of idol worship and nominal devotion to Yahweh—and in true Minion fashion—Israel displayed a desire to worship what was familiar: what they could see with their eyes and touch with their hands.

It's difficult to understand how Israel could have abandoned such a present God so quickly. They'd been rescued and set free. With their own eyes, they had watched Him destroy the last vestiges of their life of oppression. Why did they turn so fast?

We are quick to take silence as absence—to interpret a lack of desired action for abandonment. The book of Exodus hums with Eden's chorus as the Israelites turned on the One who had delivered them. The song that floated about the camp that day is the same one that I sang when the God who rescued and daily sanctifies me seemed to be silent: "You are not enough for me, Lord. I need something more." Often when we sing our discontented song, we are working out ways to construct a plan that we like better than God's.

I did not pray for contentment while I waited. I did not pray for a submissive heart that trusted God no matter what. No, I demanded what I wanted and nothing less. When He did not give me what I asked for, when He asked me to wait, when He was silent, I resolved to take care of it myself and chased after it relentlessly. Though the pursuit brought me nothing but misery and bitterness, I pressed down the memories of God's past goodness to me, and I worshiped my desires rather than the One whom I was made to worship. My idol wasn't a calf made of jewelry, but it might as well have been for all the help that my burning desire of motherhood brought me.

### Purpose in Wandering

I've always believed God to be both sovereign *and* good, but seeing Him as such in my circumstances has felt confusing at times. Was God both sovereign and good in withholding the blessing of children from me? In the early years of my infertility, I equated God's goodness with "good" circumstances—not with God Himself. In my head, God's goodness depended on His willingness to answer my prayer in the way that I wanted. But that's idolatry, and it isn't limited to my desire to have a child.

Anything that you think you need in order to believe that God is good—that's your golden calf. What we lack often becomes the object of our worship. For me it was a child, respect, and peace. For Israel it was food, victory, and a constant awareness of the plan. For you, maybe it's a spouse, a job, a mended relationship, fame, or control over your life. The tantalizing thing about idolatry is that anything fits.

Here's what is true: God is good because He is God. The circumstances that He allows in your life do not negate His goodness. Rather, they are assembled in such a way as to give Him glory for His goodness! The struggle lies in how we *respond* to those plans of His that don't make us feel immediately happy.

The Israelites give us much to learn from and identify with. When the land that God promised to give them didn't seem safe enough, they refused to settle there. They feared the occupants of the land more than they trusted God. In response to their disbelief, God sent them wandering in the desert for forty years.

Was God good in allowing Israel to circle the wilderness for four decades? How was His purpose both sovereign and good when he closed the door of the promised land to an entire generation? Though their disbelief came with long-term repercussions, God was still good to them, and He demonstrated this in many ways. In the desert of discipline, Israel harvested the fruit of His regular presence: their clothes never wore out, their shoes withstood four decades of walking, and they always had the food that they needed. During the anguish of waiting, God was teaching them to trust Him. There was reason for them to praise Him in the wilderness—for His preservation, His provision, His *presence*. He wasn't the gods of Egypt that they had worshiped in futility. The presence of Israel's one, true God meant something. His presence was for their good.

Every painful piece of our lives on earth is an opportunity for us to love Him and be loved by Him—to know He is with us and to enjoy His nearness even in sorrow. I so desperately wish I had grasped this truth in the barren years of my sanctification. Many years removed from it, I am still barely eking out an understanding of the depth of which those things are true. Life is not what we map it out to be but what God wrings from it for His glory. Even our desires for good things must be submitted to our satisfaction in God.

The Israelites craved the familiarity of their Egyptian slavery rather than God's presence in the wilderness. Similarly, I turned a blind eye to the true hunger of my heart and instead pinned my hopes on the one thing I couldn't have. We can burn ourselves down in our perpetual pursuit of desires, while never considering that sating one specific desire was never the point. Tozer said, "The way to deeper knowledge of God is through the lonely valleys of soul poverty and abnegation of all things. The blessed ones who possess the kingdom are they who have repudiated every external thing and have rooted from their hearts all sense of possessing."[1]

If the Lord brings us to a wilderness, we must strive to see it as an opportunity to learn that He is enough. Even when we are lacking, He is sovereign and good.

## What We Learn in Wandering

During forty wandering years, God's people scraped an odd, flaky substance off the ground every morning except for the Sabbath. They ate this manna every single day, because God provided it every single day. He was with them, knew what they needed, and provided for them. He made it clear that they could gather only enough for each day, or else it would rot with maggots and worms. They were permitted to gather extra only when they were preparing for the Sabbath—their day of rest. And so, until they came to the promised land of Canaan, they learned to rely on the Lord's provision of manna each morning (see Ex. 16:35).

Through this, God taught Israel trust and obedience on a daily basis. Each morning the people had to decide if He was enough for them. Stockpiling manna was futile; hoarding was an expression of fear and mistrust. If God promised daily bread, then there was no need for the people to stockpile. Except on the Sabbath, they could not borrow from yesterday's provision. Trusting God for the daily provision of what *He* knew they needed wasn't just survival. It was acknowledging His presence and knowing that it was enough.

1. A. W. Tozer, *The Pursuit of God: The Human Thirst for the Divine* (1948; repr., Camp Hill, PA: Christian Publications, 1993), 23.

We aren't scraping manna off the ground ourselves, but God has given us what we need in order to be confident in His nearness. Enjoying God's presence doesn't look like sitting quietly in a room and imagining that He's near. It's not concentrating really hard so you can somehow "feel" His presence. In addition to the gift of His Spirit (whom we will discuss much more in chapter 8), God has given us all that we need to know of Him—for this life—in Scripture. We could try to subsist on something else, but only Scripture can feed our faith—because only Scripture is given to us as nourishment.

As a pastor's wife who had been raised in a Christian home, I knew this as well as anyone. Yet I resisted God because I wanted something else. The Word of God is like manna—it's daily nourishment, daily reminders of God's nearness. It's what God knows we need in order to thrive. But, so often, we hunger for something more. I did.

In denying myself the presence of God through time in His Word, I fed my bitterness and starved my affections for God. There was manna on the ground, but I brushed off His morning mercies in search of ways to answer my own prayer. Charts, herbs, schedules, medications, tests, research—all the things that I had in my arsenal to fix my problem and achieve my dream failed me. I thought I could force myself through a door that God had not opened. No matter how I fought Him, He would always win. During all my years of infertility, I never once conceived.

But there is kindness in the Lord's closed doors. Giving me what I thought I wanted would have robbed me of what I needed most: Him. I had not abandoned faith in Him, but I lacked joy because I desired something more than Him. My prideful attempt to rule my life eventually eroded. I despaired of having a child. There was nothing left for me but to turn to the One who could answer my prayer but hadn't. I had to pick up the manna off the ground—had to swallow what God knew I needed the most.

I had to go to the Scriptures. Where else could I go? Sometimes I think that was entirely the point.

## Remember the Wandering

When we recount God's faithfulness in the past, it's easy to see why He alone deserves our worship. Scripture often models for us the practice of intentionally remembering His steadfast love. God's people were quick to run after other masters whenever following Yahweh seemed costly or strange. Remembering that God has always been trustworthy in the past helps us to trust Him with the future. For that very reason, God had the people preserve two quarts of manna in the ark of testimony as a reminder to future generations of His daily provision.

In Exodus and Leviticus, the theme of God's presence is threaded throughout the meticulous lists and unusual instructions for worship and work. The promise that He will dwell among His people is nearly always coupled with a reminder about what He has already done for the people. He reminds them over and over that He is the one who brought them out of Egypt, delivering them from slavery.

We can trace the act of remembering all throughout the Old Testament. Festivals and rituals were established in the book of Leviticus so that future generations would know of God's past faithfulness. Remembering God's past faithfulness helps us to believe in His future faithfulness. In his book *Future Grace*, John Piper writes,

> God himself commands this pattern of remembering bygone grace for the sake of faith in future grace. In Isaiah 46:9 he says, "Remember the former things long past, for I am God, and there is no other; I am God, and there is no one like Me." The reason God wants them to look back on "the former things" is to

increase their confidence in the future things he is planning for them. "My purpose will be established, and I will accomplish all My good pleasure" (Isa. 46:10). Remembering the former things that God has done gives a good foundation for believing his Word when he says, "I will accomplish all My good pleasure."[2]

This command to remember is purposeful. God knew how strong the pull would be for the people to run after the false gods of surrounding nations. He gave them a framework for living that would encourage them to keep telling the story of their deliverance by His power. In telling the story, they would remember. In Deuteronomy 6, the people are commanded to remember what God has done by speaking of it often to the next generation. They're instructed to

> be careful not to forget the LORD who brought you out of the land of Egypt, out of the place of slavery.... When your son asks you in the future, "What is the meaning of the decrees, statutes, and ordinances, which the LORD our God has commanded you?" tell him, "We were slaves of Pharaoh in Egypt, but the LORD brought us out of Egypt with a strong hand. Before our eyes the LORD inflicted great and devastating signs and wonders on Egypt, on Pharaoh, and on all his household, but He brought us from there in order to lead us in and give us the land that He swore to our fathers. The LORD commanded us to follow all these statutes and to fear the LORD our God for our prosperity always and for our preservation, as it is today. Righteousness will be ours if we are careful to follow every one of these commands before the LORD our God, as He has commanded us." (vv. 12, 20–25)

2. John Piper, *The Purifying Power of Living by Faith in Future Grace* (Sisters, OR: Multnomah Books, 1995), 103.

Celebrating Passover every year helped them to remember, but I imagine that the story—a story of great wonders and deliverance—was also told and retold with regularity around tables and campfires, at festivals and on journeys. And this practice of remembering shouldn't stop with the Israelites. Looking back is how we remember that God's presence is enough for us. We see it in Jesus at the cross.

At the cross, our sins are forgiven, our lives are redeemed, and we who were far off are brought near. The cross reconciles all that was broken in the garden by making a way for us to know God through faith in Christ. The fact that we can enjoy His presence at all is because He made a way for us to do so through Jesus. And, what's more, the gospel isn't just for salvation; it is also for our sanctification—for our growth in godliness. Remembering God's deliverance prevents us from circling our own personal deserts of bitterness. We've been reconciled so that we can know the presence that was lost in the garden.

Perhaps the Israelites were still learning God's character, and that's why they struggled to trust Him. You and I didn't get to see Him in thundering, glorious fire and smoke—but we have the rest of the story. We have access to the Father, by grace, through faith in Christ. We have every reason to eradicate the song of dissatisfaction from our repertoire. But, like Israel, we struggle to understand why God would allow us to wander in a wilderness of lack. While we demand that He answer our prayers with what we want, His reply is to remind us *who He is*. Every page of Scripture tells us who He is and what He's done. Wandering is a gift that helps us to remember this.

## The Gift of Wandering

After several years of infertility, my golden calf fell apart in another doctor's office. Words like "never" and "unlikely" and "not optimistic" filled the room with despair. I begged for God to do something with the shards of my broken dreams. And yet I was surprised to feel relief after my idol crumbled—for beneath the rubble lay a different way for me to watch the Lord work wonders. With a mixture of fear and hope, I promised to trust Him when I signed an adoption application with a shaky hand. I was not in control. This had not been my plan. And what kindness God lavished on me by giving me what *He* knew was good!

Six months later, I held my son for the very first time. In many ways, he is a story of God's faithfulness that I love to tell. Even when I rebelled, the Lord did not forget me. Had the Lord not pried my hands from my idol of fertility, I would have never known the joy of accepting the provision God had chosen for us. This child was manna in the wilderness, water from a rock, glory in the desert. The preceding years of silence were a necessary part of the story—of learning that gifts are reminders of the Giver. Though I did not see it, His presence sustained me while I waited.

My son was a precious gift that I did not deserve; yet, as I stepped into the motherhood I had yearned for, I realized that we must not bow down to our answered prayers. The fragility of a new baby revealed that I couldn't stake my eternal joy on the child I had prayed for; I had to stake it on the One I prayed to. The weight of your heart's satisfaction can't be laid on another human being or a particular outcome. Only the Giver of gifts can stand up to the heart's relentless desire to be satisfied.

It's tempting to look at an answered prayer and decide that *now* you can believe God is good. Whatever we attach to our desire for Him is still a golden calf. Though God was good in answering my plea for a child, He would have still been good if the cradle had remained empty. His goodness does not hinge on our fulfilled desires. Our desires are fulfilled when they are hinged on our enjoyment of His good character.

When you remember the ways God has sustained you, do the

stories you tell about these times focus on God's presence or on a favorable outcome? The gifts are not the end in themselves; they are meant to remind us who God is and what He has done for us, just as His provisions in the wilderness did for Israel. Whether it's the gift of answered prayer or the continual lack of it, we should remember who God is and how He has sustained us. It is always His character to be enough.

## Discussion Questions

1. "Anything that you think you need in order to believe that God is good—that's your golden calf." How can a deferred hope, even for something good, morph into idolatry?

2. How do you reconcile both the fact that God is sovereign and the fact that He is good, even when your circumstances don't seem good?

3. Think of a time when you struggled with bitterness or jealousy toward others while you waited for the Lord to answer your prayer. How can we fight for transparency and kindness to others when we are hurting?

4. The Israelites wandered in a desert for forty years as they learned to trust God. How can the areas of lack in our lives teach us to trust Him?

5. Share some of the ways God has been faithful to you in the past. Do they focus on God's presence or on a favorable outcome or both?

# 3

# A Place to Dwell

*It would seem that our Lord finds our desires not too strong, but too weak. . . . We are far too easily pleased.*

—C. S. Lewis

Sometimes, even when our prayers are answered, we don't know how to live on the other side of them. Even when the Lord intervenes and changes a frustrating situation for the better, we can still doubt Him at the next turn in our circumstances. We finally get the job, the relationship, the family, the healing—and yet we still find reasons to think that God might fail us tomorrow. We set our sights on tangible things that we think will make us happy— one right after the other—trying to achieve eternal joy through temporary measures. The trouble is not that our hearts are filled with longing. As C. S. Lewis said, the trouble is that we are too easily satisfied by poor substitutions.[1]

On the brink of an entirely new life as the free people of Yahweh, Israel struggled to trust that same Yahweh with their future. They'd followed Him through a fractured sea, watched Him

1. See C. S. Lewis, *The Weight of Glory: and Other Addresses* (1949; repr., New York: HarperOne, 2001), 26.

sweep away their enemies, and witnessed His pillar of cloud and fire. They had seen God in His power and fearsome majesty as He cloaked Mount Sinai in thunder, lightning, and smoke. They'd felt the ground beneath them shake with His presence.

But for four hundred years, generations of Israelites had been born and buried in Egyptian chains. While Moses spent a month on top of Mount Sinai taking down God's instructions for them, Israel longed for the familiar ways of work and worship. Their hands may not have been bound, but their hearts still were.

## The Burning Bush Revisited

While the Israelites were bowing down before a conglomeration of earrings and bracelets, God made a promise to them on the mountain. He told Moses, "They are to make a sanctuary for Me so that I may dwell among them" (Ex. 25:8). He gave specific instructions for what this sanctuary would look like, which included directions for building the ark of the testimony where He would keep His promise to be present. "I will meet with you there above the mercy seat, between the two cherubim that are over the ark of the testimony; I will speak with you from there about all that I command you regarding the Israelites" (Ex. 25:22). From the ark to the altar for burnt offerings down to the tassels on the priestly garments, God's detailed instructions left no questions about the order and operations of the sanctuary.

No wonder Moses was exasperated when he came down the mountain to find that the Israelites had turned so quickly away from the God he had been speaking with for the past forty days. They'd abandoned the reverent fear they had felt weeks before and moved on.

To demonstrate the foolishness of worshiping an object made from jewelry, fire, and impatience, Moses incinerated the calf, ground it into a powder, and scattered it over the people's drinking water. They tasted the bitterness of their sin with every swallow. With the residue of idolatry lingering on their lips, the Israelites were at the mercy of the God they had doubted. Would He keep His promises to them even though they were quick to defect?

In frustration and desperation, Moses turned to God, and God responded with beautiful simplicity:

Moses: "Look, You have told me, 'Lead this people up,' but You have not let me know whom You will send with me. You said, 'I know you by name, and you have also found favor in My sight.' Now if I have indeed found favor in Your sight, please teach me Your ways, and I will know You and find favor in Your sight. Now consider that this nation is Your people."

God: "My presence will go with you, and I will give you rest."

Moses: "If Your presence does not go, don't make us go up from here. How will it be known that I and Your people have found favor in Your sight unless You go with us? I and Your people will be distinguished by this from all the other people on the face of the earth."

God: "I will do this very thing you have asked, for you have found favor in My sight, and I know you by name." (Ex. 33:12–17, author's formatting)

Moses asked for *how*, but God answered with *who*. And who is what Moses needed. "I will go with you, and I will give you rest." There was no next step without those powerful words. As He had at the burning bush, God would display His power in the weakness of men. As Moses again faced the difficult task of leading God's people, God reminded Moses that *I Am*—that His presence was the way through, that His presence was enough for Moses.

Even when the people insisted that God's next steps for them were too dangerous to obey, even when the majority of the men who were sent to spy out the promised land gave a report that overshadowed God's sufficiency, even when the consequences for unbelief meant that the promise would skip a generation—even so, the *who* mattered more than the *how* or the *why*. Wandering in a desert is pointless unless you are shadowed by a holy God.

I picture the Israelites standing at the edge of a high cliff. Stretching out in front of them is miles and years of land to traverse. They had roughly forty years to learn to live as the people of Yahweh in the desert so that their children would know how to live as the people of Yahweh in the promised land (see Num. 14:28–35).

Perhaps it seems excessive for God to discipline the people by having them wander the wilderness for four decades. I believe, though, that He intended good from the consequences for their perpetual doubt. He was showing them that they were not who they used to be under Egypt's oppression. Now they belonged to Him and must reflect the fact that Yahweh's people were not like the rest of the world, who were entangled in the worship of false gods. God was also teaching them that it was dangerous to disobey Him. He was keeping them a bit desperate. He was keeping them by His side. If I've learned anything in my life as a follower of Jesus, it's that *desperate* is not a bad place to be. Desperation can cultivate deep dependence on God.

## On the Other Side of Answered Prayer

As we settled into parenthood after years of infertility, I was certain that the aching in my heart would cease. Our son was the brightest spot of joy in an incredibly difficult season of local church ministry. During the years preceding our son's birth and adoption, our church ministry had reached discouraging levels of contention. Naturally, I thought I would be content when our ministry started to look less like a failure and more like a success to our small community. Again, I hitched my joy to circumstances that I could never control.

When my husband and I walked into our church at the tender ages of twenty-seven and twenty-four, we didn't realize that we were commandeering a sinking ship. Armed with youthful inexperience and a passion for biblical literacy, we managed to set the sinking ship on fire—and not in a good way. It was hard to know which problem to address first: the fact that the ship was sinking or the fact that it was on fire.

Only a couple of months after our arrival, our rural church began a long implosion. People left for all sorts of reasons, but mostly people left because other people left. Fear got underneath everyone's skin, and we became a people of suspicion. After several years of emptying pews and internal dysfunction, our church body was a fraction of what it had been when we arrived—and not just numerically speaking. The little thread that had knit us together had nearly unraveled completely.

I turned inward in order to stay safe. *That's okay,* I told myself. *I don't need people I can't trust. I'm doing just fine in my family.* But I wasn't doing just fine. I was miserable. Lonely, bitter, and hurt, I built a wall around my home and my heart. A few short years in local church ministry had taught me one thing: the people I shared a pew with had the greatest potential to hurt me. I figured that if they couldn't get past the wall I was building, then they couldn't hurt me. The wall grew steadily—bricked with bitterness and sealed with suspicion.

I thought we were called to this small church in this small town in order to be successful—to show how ministry was properly done. We thought we could bail out the ship in the nick of time with our academic prowess and our background in healthy church ministry. We had come with dreams of fixing the church up right.

But actually we came so that our dreams could die. We came to learn what humility looked like. We came to experience the odd freedom that comes in failure. If we'd experienced anything more than failure, we would have grabbed the glory. There was no room in our failures for glory-grabbing—and rightly so. No, we came to sacrifice the grand ideas we had brought with us. We came to this church in this town because God had refining work to do in our church. And in us.

### Tabernacles and Late-Night Meetings

Just before Israel's wilderness wandering, God had His people build a tabernacle—a tent that could be set up and torn down whenever the Lord moved the people through the desert in their travels. Don't miss what's happening here! God instructed them to build a place for Him to *live with them*—right in the middle of their tribal arrangements in the camp. All of Israel could watch His glory settle as a cloud over the holiest room of the tabernacle. No one would be able to deny His presence among them. This wasn't man's attempt to find God, nor was it the result of a plot hatched by Moses to manipulate God into being present among the people. No, the whole thing was God's idea. He would dwell with His people; and, since they were sinful, He would provide both His presence and a way for them to enjoy it.

The tabernacle was a bloody place designed for the implementation of their sacrificial system. Since the day that Adam and Eve swallowed the fruit of discontent, reconciliation with God has required atonement for sin. The priests in the tabernacle offered sacrifices to pay for the sins of man, because the sins of man continued to multiply. On and on it went. The bleating of sheep and the lowing of cattle before the slaughter cried out for another way. That was the point. The altar was spattered with blood—stained with humanity's deep need for rescue.

Every complaint in the wilderness, every longing to go back, every grumbling for God to do things differently called for the slaughter of something more than sheep and cattle. The people didn't believe that God was enough for them, but He lived among them in order to prove that He was. Every time He revealed their need for provision, atonement, and guidance, He supplied for the need Himself. In the tabernacle, God showed the people how desperate they were for absolution. In His carefully constructed tent, He taught them to obey and live. When the living God dwells among you, you have everything you need.

Every instruction in the tent was a sign, a preparation, an arrow for what was coming. Even the priests were copies of a better Priest to come. They would all point to Jesus. "These serve as a copy and shadow of the heavenly things," wrote the author of Hebrews, ". . . but Jesus has now obtained a superior ministry, and to that degree He is the mediator of a better covenant, which has been legally enacted on better promises" (Heb. 8:5–6). Yes, even in Exodus—even in the institution of the sacrificial system that would atone for sins—God was preparing the way for Jesus.

> Every priest stands day after day ministering and offering the same sacrifices time after time, which can never take away sins. But this man, after offering one sacrifice for sins forever, sat down at the right hand of God. (Heb. 10:11–12)

In Exodus, God doled out the directions for the tabernacle's construction to Moses on top of the mountain *while* the people were down in the valley on their knees before a golden calf. His continual plan to dwell among His people wasn't just in spite of their sin but *because* of it.

Written into His plans for the tabernacle is His certain, steadfast love.

I will dwell among the Israelites and be their God. And they will know that I am Yahweh their God, who brought them out of the land of Egypt, so that I might dwell among them. I am Yahweh their God. (Ex. 29:45–46)

There should have been no doubt in their minds that Yahweh was with them. We might not equate presence with steadfast love, but we should.

Is there any better way for God to love us than to be with us? His presence is the deepest need we have. That the almighty God would bend so low as to be with us in our grief, our sin, our confusion, and our doubt is at odds with every other type of man/god relationship that has ever been conceived. This is steadfast love, *checed*, the peculiar kind of love He displays with His nearness to His people. He does not abandon them in their suffering but loves them by being with them through their adversity. The Psalms are filled with praise for the steadfast love that God maintains for His people. Often the psalmists connect this love to His promises to keep His word to them (see Pss. 89:28; 115:1). God's presence is the expression of love that we have always needed and a promise that He has always kept.

God's plan to redeem us is sewn with threads of nearness—even flesh-and-blood nearness. His way of redemption was designed for the purpose of His glory and our enjoyment of His presence. We are the ones who wreck the good plans. Our sin prevents us from enjoying His presence perfectly, and we foolishly try to fix it with something besides Him. *Anything* besides Him. It is always futile, always empty, always a false start.

The disciplines of confession and repentance, and the practices of worship and atonement, displayed the depth of Israel's need for Yahweh. Being tethered to the sacrificial system revealed their profound helplessness to reconcile themselves to God. They couldn't do it themselves. The blood of animals could barely do it on a temporary basis. Maybe they thought they didn't deserve to wander for forty years. Maybe they found the practice of substitutionary atonement to be excessive. Maybe they didn't see it. But because we have the entirety of Scripture, we can see it.

Since we sit on the other side of the cross, we can see how God scraped away Israel's layers of ingrained idolatry and taught them the posture of absolute dependence on Him. He does the same thing in my life with every trial, with every broken dream, with every sin ensnaring my heart. I realize it with every painful recognition that I cannot answer my own needs. Look at your unmet longings. Look at how you've tried to answer them. Could God be using them to keep you near to Him? What if there's a sovereign goodness in the desperation that you feel?

"Does the LORD take pleasure in burnt offerings and sacrifices as much as in obeying the LORD? Look: to obey is better than sacrifice, to pay attention is better than the fat of rams" (1 Sam. 15:22). God doesn't mind if we're desperate. He'd rather have us be that way than complacent. Desperation can lead to obedience. When we've exhausted every avenue, God can use our desperation to lead us down the path of obedience.

> You do not want a sacrifice, or I would give it;
> You are not pleased with a burnt offering.
> The sacrifice pleasing to God is a broken spirit.
> God, You will not despise a broken and humbled heart. (Ps.
>    51:16–17)

It's what He desires: desperation and obedience, brokenness and a yielded spirit.

Obedient. Broken. Humbled. It's so backward! It's so countercultural. Doesn't God want us to be strong and happy? Doesn't He want us to feel secure in our abilities? No. He wants us to rely on Him, and so He uses our desperation to that end. Once it's uncovered, the desperation that lives in all our hearts lays the path to Him. When He scrapes away our layers of self-worship and me-centered idolatry, we see that the holes in our life plans are pretense. They're desires masquerading as needs. Desperation lays bare our real need. The yearning, the discontent—it all leads back to Him. That's what it's for.

Every yearning that presses against your chest is for this purpose—to find satisfaction in God. Jim Elliot wrote, "There is within a hunger after God, given of God, filled by God."[2] Since we are too easily satisfied, sometimes He lets us get desperate so that we will see the need beneath our unfulfilled desires.

Medicating every ache with the stuff of earth clouds our vision—keeps us from recognizing that the true, deep source of the ache is our longing for the One who made us. So when the Lord pulls the rug out from under our temporary fixes, the ache swells and burns and leads us to consider the real cure. Suffering, trials, unfulfilled desires—He may use what hurts to expose what's underneath. If you're feeling desperate because of your unfulfilled desires, consider what God may be doing. His faithful love exposes the real need so that He can meet it with His nearness.

*Desperate* is the perfect word to describe how I felt as we went down with that burning, sinking ship we called *church*. My uncertainty swelled beneath the pressure of late nights that I spent on the couch waiting for my husband to return from meetings where reports of his failures were brought to him with equal parts glee and grudge. I would watch the minutes tick by on the living-room clock while I waited for the familiar sound of my husband's truck lumbering down the driveway. I would listen closely to the slamming of the truck door. If William was humming or singing, then the meeting had been bearable. If I couldn't detect a sound from

2. Quoted in Elisabeth Elliot, *Shadow of the Almighty: The Life and Testament of Jim Elliot* (1958; repr., New York: HarperCollins Publishers, 1979), 60.

the door slam until the jingle of his house key in the back-door lock, then I knew another bomb had gone off and we'd be up all night pulling bits of shrapnel from his heart.

Each late night that I waited for his arrival, I would sit on the couch with a sick stomach and my Bible while I prayed the Lord's protection over my husband. I didn't know what else to do. The burning in my side, the knot in my throat, the panic in my chest welled up in me each time. Nothing in my arsenal of problem-solving had ever fixed any of the broken parts of our lives, so I thought of Peter, who said to Jesus, "Where else can we go? You have the words of eternal life!" (see John 6:68). I'd exhausted my options. I was as desperate as I'd ever been for God to be near. There is no substitution for posturing yourself before the living God with your lips forming the words *help me*. There is no better, lower place.

Like a wandering Hebrew slave longing for Egypt's certainty, I walked in circles until desperation got to me. Finally, I turned to the Word. I practiced the plan that was laid out in Scripture. I confessed. I remembered the gospel. I remembered how I had been brought near to God because of Christ's once-and-for-all sacrifice at the cross. I repented of my fear even as the Lord met me in it. I combed through the Scriptures for help. Where else could I go? Who else had the words of life but my Savior?

God was near when I prayed on the beige couch in our living room—the first brand-new piece of furniture we had acquired. It took us a year to pay it off. I sit on it every morning now to read my Bible and drink my coffee. It's stained and worn. It sinks in too deeply and carries the memories of the nights I sat cross-legged and crying. The God of Israel's wilderness met me on that couch. He whispered from the pages of my Bible, "I am with you always" (Matt. 28:20); "I will never leave you or forsake you" (Heb. 13:5); "[My] faithful love is constant" (Ps. 52:1). He might as well have been sitting on the beige couch cushion next to me—He was *that* near. And this is what He communicated in the glory that settled over the tent in the wilderness: He was different from the lifeless, pagan gods of yesterday and the mind-numbing distractions of today. He came to His people because they were helpless to rightly come to Him.

If He would meet me on a beige couch when His Word was all I had, then His presence really would be sufficient for my every next turn. God was teaching me to come to Him with every ugly thought, every vengeful desire, every demand for vindication. He may not answer us in the ways that we want, but He can teach us the steps of obediently coming to Him anyway. In our bleakest seasons of uncertainty, God is near. When we struggle to obey, He is near. When we're desperate, He is near. Perhaps it feels like wandering, but desperate obedience is the training ground for trust.

## You Move, We Move

It was a study of obedience, really. Israel moved when He moved; they stayed when He stayed. All the ways that God structured the ordinances of the sacrificial system—the feasts and festivals, the grain and restitution offerings, the moving forward and the staying put—were all an exercise in obedience for Israel. "Whether it was two days, a month, or longer, the Israelites camped and did not set out as long as the cloud stayed over the tabernacle. But when it was lifted, they set out. They camped at the Lord's command, and they set out at the Lord's command" (Num. 9:22–23).

I knew of a young woman who lived with some friends while she got back on her feet after her incarceration. She had come to faith in Christ in prison but struggled to remain faithful to Him after her release. Her old addictions and self-destructive behaviors, which had been physically suppressed in prison, resurfaced in her freedom, and her life over the next decade was a cycle of relapse, rehab, prison, and release. She didn't know how to live free in both body and soul.

For Israel, as for this young woman, freedom produced temptations they couldn't have imagined while circling the desert and waiting for God to give the okay for tabernacle deconstruction. God's clearly delineated laws and instructions were meant to help Israel live freely in safety. Wherever Israel was in their journey, the Lord was with them. The closing words of Exodus read, "For the cloud of the LORD was over the tabernacle by day, and there was a fire inside the cloud by night, visible to the entire house of Israel throughout all the stages of their journey" (Ex. 40:38). At every step, He assured them of His presence so that they could trust Him.

A generation passed before the people were permitted to enter the land that had been promised to Abraham, Isaac, and Jacob. It was the children, now grown, who stepped into the land of milk and honey—a haven that the parents had dreamed of while subsisting on morning mercies and manna. After kicking up four decades of desert dust, the last of the golden-calf worshipers had died.

Some of the younger generation no doubt remembered their first dry crossing when God had held back the waters of the Red Sea so they could pass through to safety. Maybe Joshua remembered. He was Israel's next leader, who was ushered into the promised land along with Caleb by virtue of his good report of the land and the way he took the Lord at His word. A second crossing through a body of water proved that God would make good on His promise to be with Joshua, just as He had been with Moses.

The people of God could see His glory with their own eyes— but as they began a life in the promised land, they struggled to trust this God who had sustained them. The similarities between God's people then and now isn't lost on me. He accomplishes marvelous things in our lives and answers prayers we had nearly given up on, and yet we question Him at every next turn. When we feel like we're circling a desert and fumbling for obedience, we should view this as a training ground for trusting God with every next step. A decade in the wilderness is a gift if the Lord is with you. Desperate obedience might be exactly where the Lord wants you to be, so He can teach you that He is enough.

## Discussion Questions

1. In Exodus 33, Moses expressed his hesitancy and fear over leading God's stubborn people. Read verses 12–18. What was so reassuring about God's promise to Moses? Explain why knowing *who* might be better than knowing *how*.

2. In His kindness and providence, sometimes God answers our prayers in the way that we hope. How do we prevent these answered prayers from taking the place of the One whom we pray to in our hearts?

3. In Numbers 28–29, the Lord gave Israel numerous commands regarding the number and kinds of sacrifices for sin. Read Hebrews 10:1–14. Why did God institute the sacrificial system if those sacrifices for sin would never be enough? What was He preparing His people for?

4. "Is there any better way for God to love us than to be with us?" How does the story of Scripture display God's faithful love to His people?

5. How does desperation make us depend on God? How can dependence lead us to obedience?

# 4

# The King We Need

*Of the flesh and its false emotions I have quite had
my fill. Of Jesus I cannot seem to get enough.*

—JIM ELLIOT

In the mornings, I have the very spiritual ritual of hitting the
snooze button one too many times before heading straight to
the coffee pot. Cup in hand, I open the blinds to let in the weak
morning light before settling on my couch with my Bible. I riffle
through the promises of God and the jumbled state of my heart
while the sun comes up behind the tulip trees in my backyard, its
light filtering through their branches. I glance from the branchy
sunlight to the blurry words of my Bible. Always a tiny voice whispers of the warmth of my bed—the allure of a few more minutes
of sleep. But always the Lord is with me as I sit and watch the sun
rise—which it does with even less reliability than the mercies He
pours into my lap.

I search the Word. I run my finger down the list of all the
things I pray for—things God has promised; things I am desperate for. That routine complete, I move to the front of my house
with my coffee and watch my neighbors perform their own
morning rituals. One neighbor comes out in his bathrobe for the

newspaper while his dog stands in the street, barking and inhibiting traffic. Another neighbor (and friend) walks the block in her work clothes and heels with her dog before heading to the office. The older couple on the corner is fully dressed by dawn, watching the neighborhood wake up from their porch.

These rituals, these predictable procedures, are expressions of what we believe—no matter how small or seemingly insignificant they may be. They show us what we value. How we prioritize our habits speaks of what matters to us. Have you ever wondered why people of faith rise early to read an ancient book? What is to be gained from lost sleep and old words?

It's been years since those nights of stomachaches and desperation, when I waited on the couch for my husband to come home from his weekly flagellations. Trouble has been reborn dozens of times since then, under other monikers: doubt, disease, physical pain, betrayal. But I'm still tethered to those nights, and I'm glad. What keeps me connected to those early days of ministerial strife is the way the Lord ministered to me through His presence. When every good plan was met with resistance, when our zeal was mistaken for impatience, when we didn't know what we were doing, when we repeatedly picked up the pieces of a broken church who didn't quite trust us, God made Himself known to me through His words.

I didn't know that God was working something good with the betrayal I felt while I was sitting silently through bizarre church meetings. I couldn't grasp that He was wringing beauty from the way my disease-ridden abdomen still ached with emptiness. He was tethering me to Himself. He was opening my eyes to my perpetual state of neediness. Up until the doctor said the word *infertility*, up until the ministry blew up, up until loneliness threatened to swallow me whole, I didn't understand that I was needy.

We try to quiet our need with food and drink, music and books, relationships and possessions. None of these things feel like the wrong answer—until we wake up one morning and realize that we're self-medicating our yearnings with created things. In the middle of the night, when nothing else can heal the pain of betrayal or loneliness, we can only go to the One who knows it all.

I sit with my Bible in my lap every morning because I know that if I don't, I'll keep trying to answer the questions in my life with created things instead of the Creator. Remembering who He is and what He's done keeps us near His side. The One who made us to need Him is the only One who can meet our needs. When all the things that we use to answer our longings fail us, desperation shatters our golden calves. The Word reminds us that all we have is the Lord—and that He is all we need.

## Dangerous Forgetfulness

The generation of Israelites who reached the promised land had known only a nomadic life. God raised up Joshua to take Moses's place and renewed His covenant with Israel so they would know exactly how to live a non-nomadic life. He commanded them to remember the past so they would know who He is and how far He had brought them. Remembering His past faithfulness kept them tethered to His side. They would always be better off when they were aware of their need for Him.

Relying on Him meant that they were protected by His sovereign goodness. "Remember that I chose you," He says often in Deuteronomy, in contexts such as Deuteronomy 9:6: "not . . . because of your righteousness, for you are a stiff-necked people." It was Yahweh who kept them alive for those forty years in the wild. "The Lord your God has been with you this past 40 years, and you have lacked nothing" (Deut. 2:7).

The book of Joshua recounts all the ways that God kept His promises to give the land of Canaan to the people of Israel. There is the memorable story of the falling walls of Jericho and the fiercely tenacious Rahab. There's the day that the sun stood still during a battle, when more men fell because of the Lord's actions than because of any skill or weapon of the Israelite army. Renewed covenant, new land—all was ready for their next stage of living like the people of Yahweh to begin.

God had ingrained reminders of His faithfulness to Israel into their every festival, rite, and routine. He sewed His name into the rhythms of their daily lives, because He knew how easily they would forget—not because He was forgettable, but because a craving for something besides Yahweh was imprinted on the hearts of every human after Eden. Forgetting was the enemy.

The end of Joshua's life bled into a period when Israel was known for little more than a steady moral decline. It happened because of forgetting. The very thing God had warned Israel against, they did (or didn't do, depending on how you look at it). The Israelites forgot to remember. After Joshua died, "that whole generation was also gathered to their ancestors. After them another generation rose up who did not know the LORD or the works He had done for Israel" (Judg. 2:10).

Danger creeps in when we forget who—and whose—we are. The book of Judges recounts this danger, detailing Israel's bloody, ugly downward spiral as it fought with itself and the surrounding nations. God had stopped providing daily manna. The people didn't need it—they were able to eat from the land the very first year. Maybe the new agrarian lifestyle made them want to hedge their agricultural bets and worship the god of the harvest, or maybe they wanted to worship both Yahweh and the other gods for good measure. Whatever the reason, their biggest pull into forgetfulness was idolatry.

While I cringe with each of Israel's failures to stay on the path God had so clearly set before the nation, I understand the draw to worship something tangible. It's easier to pledge yourself to something that you think you can hold, influence, or control.

Israel must have thought they could supply their own needs if they mingled idolatry with worship of Yahweh. Including other, pagan gods in their worship practices "just in case" revealed their fear of entrusting themselves to God completely. Their Creator lived among them. His presence meant He would satisfy their every need, as He'd done ever since their bonds had been broken in Egypt. Rejecting God's sufficient presence always results in idolatry. It always means worshiping something else. Israel ran after their neighbors' gods. This time, instead of signs and wonders to remind them that He was their God, He sent judgment.

A pattern emerges in the book of Judges: Israel rebels and worships false idols. God sends judgment for their idolatry because He knows it will turn their hearts toward Him. They cry out to Him in distress. He relents and forgives. They worship Him temporarily, but then the cycle repeats itself—over and over again. Israel rebels, God punishes, Israel "repents," God relents.

God showed kindness to His people during this ugly chapter of their history. Their patterns of sin were so blatant, He could have given up on them altogether. But He is slow to anger and abounding in kindness. Though Israel kept breaking their covenant to Him, He would not break His word to them. He had twelve men and one woman stand as judge at various points to provide some leadership and means of deliverance throughout the years of rebellion. Israel could not resist the allure of idolatry, and through every act of defection, they declared that Yahweh had failed them. They sought sufficiency and fullness in objects of stone and wood. Every time they bent the knee to bow to these idols, the old garden song wafted from the land of inheritance: "You are not enough for me." Every time they ran after a pagan idol, they denied that the presence of God was all they needed.

Rather than setting their hearts on the God who had led their grandfathers out of Egypt, they ran after what offered fullness faster, what was closer, what promised to give them exactly what their flesh demanded. The idols of the foreign nations were connected to empty promises: fertility, good harvests, prosperity. Rebellion against Yahweh was foolish; He had always promised to take care of His people. He lived in the midst of their camp! He would have supplied every need that they took to another god.

Judges closes on the bleakest note: "In those days there was no king in Israel; everyone did whatever he wanted" (Judg. 21:25). Oh, how the people needed a permanent rescue! And oh, how God was still planning it! Israel's disobedience would not thwart the plans He had set in motion before the foundations of the world. He had promised His presence. No matter how hard they ran or how much the consequences would hurt, God would keep His promise to be with His people, because He is who they needed. He is always what we all need.

## Dry Spells Are for Perseverance

Have you ever reached the end of a difficult season and wondered why you felt closer to the Lord when things were hard? When life evens out, do you find that your desire to cling to Christ has dissipated? The truth is that desperation is an all-weather friend. We are as desperate for the Lord's nearness on our best days as we are on our worst days. We just *know* it more on our worst days. After my ongoing years of infertility and ministry trials leveled out temporarily, I was surprised to find that trouble-free days lent themselves to a spiritual dullness. The absence of disaster wilted my desperation for the Lord's presence.

For the first several years of motherhood, I felt little emotion when I came to the Scriptures. My previously desperate, thirsty heart felt dry and brittle. There were little moments, small bursts of recognition, when a tiny cobwebbed corner of my heart lit up with a knowing. *Oh! That point in the sermon—that resonates somewhere inside.* Or *That stirring when I listened to Andrew Peterson's new album—that's familiar.* Small bursts—but mostly a spiritual existence that had lost its affection for Jesus.

You know that apathetic feeling, right? Sometimes it feels like a famine of emotion, and sometimes it feels like your aorta has become a chunk of ice beneath your sternum. Some people call it a dry spell. Every morning I dragged myself to the couch and wondered why it didn't feel like He was there. I knew He had promised to be with me, but I couldn't find Him.

I kept thumbing aimlessly through my Bible. My previous years of desperation had built the habit—but now my heart wasn't in it. Still, I plodded on. Coming cold was better than not coming at all.

It's so tempting to quit reading the Bible when it seems like nothing is sticking, isn't it? Why pray if your heart feels cold? Why persevere when the Scriptures don't seem to say anything about your situation? I get it. Years of reading the same Bible on the same couch, with the same dead feeling inside, passed me by. We'd reached the other side of answered prayers, but my heart was cold. I didn't want to follow Jesus like *this*.

But there's no in-between. Either you follow Him or you don't. You submit to His Word or you don't. Emotions are not truth-tellers, and feelings are the worst instructors. When subjected to the authority of God's Word, they can rightly express what is stirred up or grieved or affected. But they do *not* get to call the shots when it comes to following Jesus. When the feelings don't come along with the determination to obey the Lord, this is when perseverance gets to do its good work. Perseverance is plodding forward when everything in you resists.

According to James, it takes trials in order for perseverance to mature (see 1:2–4). And while you may hesitate to call a spiritual dry spell a *trial*, God may use this very season to lay the groundwork for perseverance during future trials. On every gray day of spiritual apathy that you come to Him with a cold heart, you practice perseverance. He is training you to come to Him when you don't feel like it so that you'll be sure to come to Him when life takes a hard turn. The motivation here is that, no matter how cold your heart may feel, the Lord will meet you when you come to Him in His Word. His presence is promised whether you're aware of it or not. And the more you practice coming, the more aware of His presence you'll be.

The Lord wasn't just teaching me perseverance—he was *wringing* it out of me. Extracting, wrenching, prying. He pulled perseverance out of the tiniest, most blocked-up recesses of my heart. I couldn't see it then, but He was preparing me for the darkest days ahead. He is the God who faithfully keeps His promises, and whether or not I felt like pressing on, He never ceased to be present. He doesn't waste our desperate seasons—whether they send us to the Word in desperation or dull our hearts with dryness. He can use any season to keep us close to Him.

## The Last Judge

The period of the judges ended when God raised up a prophet whom the people desperately needed. Samuel was a gift to Israel. He urged the people to return to the Lord wholeheartedly and to rid themselves of the idolatry that characterized their lives. The perpetual idol-chasing was always a symptom of Israel's doubt that God's presence was enough for them.

Under Samuel's leadership, Israel confessed their sin and removed their places of idol worship. The Lord routed their Philistine enemy, and Samuel set up a stone of remembrance because he knew that the people were inclined to forget. He wanted them to remember where their sin had led them and what it had cost. But by the end of Samuel's lifetime, the remembering fell away. Judges weren't good enough. The prophet was getting old. An uncontainable, untouchable God wasn't what the new generation in Israel had in mind.

They wanted something more than the presence in the midst of the camp. They wanted what would make them like their neighbors. They wanted the appearance of power. They wanted more than the presence of the God who lived among them. They wanted a tangible ruler. They wanted a king.

## A Tale of Two Kings, or Maybe Three

Following the Exodus and the entry into the promised land, Israel's move to a monarchy is one of the most momentous events of the Old Testament. It seems celebratory, at first. After all, God did promise way back in Genesis that someone from the family of Judah (Abraham's great-grandson) would rule Israel from the throne. It wasn't a departure from God's plan for Israel to have a king. So what is it that makes their demand for a king seem like a wrong move? The Lord is always concerned with the motives of our hearts, and in this case His people were motivated by the nations around them rather than by fear of God. They didn't ask Him for a king as much as they demanded it of Him.

To be fair, Samuel was old, and his two sons were dishonest, perverse, and unjust. Because the leadership was such a disgrace, the elders of Israel went to Samuel. What would have happened if they'd come to Samuel and said, "Samuel, we love you, but you're old. And your sons are terrible. Will you ask the Lord to show us how we can best follow Him?" Perhaps things would have turned out differently. But rather than seek the Lord, the elders demanded a king, "the same as all the other nations have" (1 Sam. 8:5). Discontent with being known as the distinct people of Yahweh who were ruled only by Yahweh, they wanted a human leader like all the other nations—nations that were known for child sacrifice and temple prostitution. The path to idolatry is paved with stones of comparison, selfishness, and impatience.

The Lord revealed to Samuel what was really going on: "They

have not rejected you; they have rejected Me as their king. They are doing the same thing to you that they have done to Me, since the day I brought them out of Egypt until this day, abandoning Me and worshiping other gods" (1 Sam. 8:7–8).

Israel's rejection of God's authority laid bare their desire to worship something else. It revealed what's underneath all our idolatrous desires: doubt that God is enough for us. It's not a lot different from when we look to social media for affirmation or when we turn to a bag of chips because we're anxious. We're much the same when we feed our anger by not forgiving a church member who has hurt us or when we imagine that our lives will be perfect when we have children, when we're thinner, when we're popular, when we're well-known and well-liked. It's not unlike the insatiable desire for pornography or power or money. "Give us a king" sounds a lot like "Fill me with something besides You, Lord." *Give us a king.* It was the countermelody to Israel's favorite song: "You are not enough for us." We like to think our idolatry is less serious because it doesn't involve a graven image, but there is no hierarchy beneath the label of idol-worshiper.

So Israel crowned their first king: Saul, of the tribe of Benjamin. Saul was an unstable and disturbing character, and Israel suffered under his rule. He was prideful, impulsive, and disobedient. He carried out plans half-heartedly unless they served himself. The king whom the Israelites had demanded failed them repeatedly. But God did not abandon His people, as Samuel reminded them. "The LORD will not abandon His people, because of His great name and because He has determined to make you His own people" (1 Sam. 12:22). He had determined to make them His own people. God goes to great lengths to assure us that He keeps His promises.

When Saul deliberately disobeyed God's instructions, his kingship unraveled. He stayed on the throne long after young David was called in from the pasture, smelling of sheep and songs and hard work, and anointed as the next king of Israel. When David, a descendent of Judah, took the throne, the people thrived under a king who feared and treasured God.

The Lord made David a promise that echoed the one He had made to David's forefather, Abraham. To David, God said, "I took you from the pasture and from following the sheep to be ruler over My people Israel. I have been with you wherever you have gone, and I have destroyed all your enemies before you" (2 Sam. 7:8–9). Of David's future son, the Lord said,

> He will build a house for My name, and I will establish the throne of his kingdom forever. . . . My faithful love will never leave him as I removed it from Saul; I removed him from your way. Your house and kingdom will endure before Me forever, and your throne will be established forever. (vv. 13, 15–16)

God was not just referring to David's son Solomon. He went many generations deep to keep this promise. The promise leaps from the worn pages of the Old Testament story: the future Son is Jesus.

## Great King David and His Greater Son

In all the ways that Saul failed as king of Israel, David excelled. He was mighty in battle, fair in judgment, and loyal to Yahweh. He ruled Israel for a good, long time—forty years. He was, in many ways, the king that Israel had originally hoped for. But he wasn't perfect by any stretch of the imagination. He had a weakness for women—a sin that is especially magnified in his adulterous relationship with Bathsheba. His sin revealed more sinful tendencies, as he sought to cover up the pregnancy that resulted from his affair.

The Lord uncovered the root of David's sin: "Now therefore,

the sword will never leave your house because you despised Me and took the wife of Uriah the Hittite to be your own wife" (2 Sam. 12:10). David had rejected Yahweh in order to pursue what he thought would fill him up. His sin took him farther than he planned to go, I'm certain. First, he failed to believe that God was enough for him. Then, that rejection blossomed into adultery and murder and resulted in a dead husband and a dead child.

His actions had far-reaching repercussions. Though David and Bathsheba had another child, David's other grown children fought and abused one another for the rest of David's rule. One son raped a half-sister. Another son had that brother killed *and* tried to usurp David's throne. The sword was ever near in David's house. However, David was not Saul. He exhibited a brand of remorse that Saul never mustered.

Many of our psalms flow from the ink of David's repentance. The king of Israel wrote incredibly transparent words about his failure to obey the Lord. He taught the Israelites to sing his poems about the devastating effects of sin and the indescribable, steadfast love of the Lord. His repentance stood between his failures and God's faithfulness. I don't know how I would have endured the darkest days of my life without the pages of David's vulnerable honesty in my Bible. When it comes to shame or grief, the Psalms are the door of the house where hope lives. As he looks forward with longing to being rescued from sin, David points us to the One who can carry all our shame and grief.

Israel's greatest king was a struggling, conflicted man who knew that he was loved by a present God. He was Israel's best hope, a filmy shadow of a descendant who would do it all so much better—who would do it best. I picture David feverishly inking out the ways in which his sin was great but his God was greater. I imagine his face ravaged by grief when he realized that he "was the man" guilty of the very sins that angered him (see 2 Sam. 12:7). I can see him lying prostrate on the ground before the Lord after the death of each of his children, knowing that he was partly to blame. That kind of grief can undo a man. Or it can put him on his face before his God. David's one constant was the never-leaving presence of God.

If I were to stand before my entire nation with my sins written down for all to read and judge, I wouldn't measure any higher than David. While David waited for Jesus, pointing to Him with every wrong and right thing he did, you and I stand on the other side of history, fully covered by the Savior who David only dimly hoped for. When he pressed his reed against the parchment and wrote about the future hope of Israel, he didn't know that the ink spilled out the name of Jesus. When he wrote about the Good Shepherd in Psalm 23, he couldn't imagine that the Shepherd would die for His sheep. When he rejoiced over the forgiveness of sins in Psalm 32, he had no inkling of how thoroughly Jesus would cover our sins. When he cried out for the Lord to rescue him, he didn't know that the Rescuer would speak his own words while carrying David's sin and your sin and my sin on His bloody shoulders. David didn't know. He only hoped.

God kept all His promises to David. He is still keeping His promises to David, though we are the beneficiaries. Great King David's greater Son Jesus paid for our sins because God promised to keep David's family on the throne forever. And in that promise is the continued promise of His presence, for Jesus would exhibit God's presence in a way that no one would have expected. If Jesus is your Savior, it's because God made promises to David. He is with you because of His promise to David. When God makes a promise, no man can thwart His plans to keep it.

## The Rhythm of Remembering

Many of David's psalms begin with doubt and end with hope. The reed in his hands may have shaken out words in fear, but when the ink dried, David was resolved to hope in the Lord who had never failed him. Often I have worked through that same pattern of lament, panic, remembrance, and resolution as I've read the Scripture. I've found that the act of remembering leads to a resolute perseverance, which we'll see more of in chapter 9.

This is why the redeemed people of God read, meditate on, and study Scripture. We need to remember who He is and what He has done in order for us to persevere in our faith. His Word is a sword that both protects and defends. Though we're tempted to settle for temporary fixes, the Word anchors us in the depths of God's sufficiency. We so quickly forget that the Lord is the one who satisfies the heart's hunger. In one breath we forget the way He has saved us.

But the Scriptures have the power to remind us where we've been, who we were, who we are now, and where we're going. This is why we rise early to meditate on His promises or spend our lunch hour studying His words. It's what draws me to the faded couch with the tulip-tree sunrise. I am more *aware* of the Lord's nearness when His words are soaking my thoughts, seeping into my mind with power and truth and memory. Remembering the past faithfulness of God ignites our faith in His present and future faithfulness. Our confidence in God's presence is kindled through our regular opening of His Word. A friend of mine who works as a firefighter calls this being "fully engulfed" in the Scriptures. Allowing the Word to engulf your heart can eventually thaw what's cold.

When our hearts struggle to absorb the Scriptures, the Word does not lose its power. When our emotions are slow to catch up to truth, the Lord doesn't abandon us. In kindness, He urges us to press on—to keep reading. Keep absorbing. Keep the rhythm of coming to the Lord with your desperation. The rhythms of remembering keep us close to His side so that we'll know where to turn when trials do come.

## Discussion Questions

1. Have you ever self-medicated your longings with created things? Give some examples of what this has looked like in your life (for example, using food to quiet your loneliness or spending money excessively to feel in control).
2. Desperation frequently drives us to the Word for relief, but sometimes spiritual dry spells keep us from it. Why is persevering in knowing God through prayer and Scripture so important, especially when we don't feel like it? Why is "coming cold" better than not coming at all?
3. Have you ever demanded something of God, the way Israel demanded a king? What are we saying about God when we make demands of Him?
4. Compare and contrast the reigns of Saul and of David. What is the difference you see between them, both when they each failed and when they each succeeded before the Lord?
5. The rhythm of remembering is one that we see in Scripture often. How does this aid us in persevering in our faith?

# 5

# Waiting in Silence

*What we experience as God's absence or distance or silence is phenomenological. It's how we perceive it. It's how at some point it looks and feels but it isn't how it is.*

—JON BLOOM

Have you ever poured your heart out in prayer and wondered whether God was listening? I mean, you know that He hears everything, but you wonder if He *heeds* anything. You pray and pray for an answer and eventually tell yourself you'd be satisfied with *any* answer, if only God would respond. You realize when you've wrestled with God in prayer that He cannot be manipulated. Silence from the heavenly realm seems like a no—and sometimes it is. Sometimes, however, silence means you need to wait. And sometimes it means you need to wait for a really long time, because God is teaching you something in the waiting.

I remember the first day I noticed the pain. It was different from my regular pain that could be temporarily diffused by surgeries. This new pain grew in small increments. It began with a prick of heat at the base of my spine one morning. I thought I'd slept at an odd angle. Maybe I needed new running shoes or a firmer mattress. The pain persisted, steadily building momentum until eventually

I wasn't just waking up with pain—I was waking up because of it. I tried stretches, chiropractic care, and Pilates. Nothing touched the ache that was spreading up my spine. I was twenty-nine years old when it began and thirty-five when I knew its name.

A host of other odd but seemingly unrelated symptoms presented themselves shortly after the pain started, but each doctor's appointment revealed picture-perfect blood work and unremarkable scans. I was the epitome of good health, it seemed. I chalked it up to stress. After all, we had decided to grow our family again by beginning the arduous process of international adoption at a time when our church still needed regular resuscitation. We split our attention between a stressful adoption process and ongoing dysfunction in our church life.

This addition of mysterious pain made me feel closed in by difficult circumstances. With new and old struggles strangling my spiritual health, I feared that I would forget the good things I had learned about God during my infertility and dry seasons. I didn't want to start over. I didn't want to wrestle with doubt about God's motives. I didn't want to be the girl in the garden, reaching for a fruit she didn't need and humming a song she shouldn't sing. I wanted to move forward, not back—but on the other end of my prayers for help seemed to be a great silence. I wanted to believe that God was with me, but the silence begged to differ. I think we all struggle to trust God when He's silent.

### A Place and a Promise

As we trace the theme of God's presence through the Old Testament time line, we see a big shift in the way God kept His promise to be present with His people. Sometimes His nearness was unmistakable—a cloud over the tabernacle—and sometimes the people were sure He had abandoned them. (He hadn't.) And, for a time, He dwelled among His people in a permanent temple.

During his reign, David expressed his desire to build this dwelling place for God. Though a noble pursuit, it wasn't the Lord's plan for David to take up that endeavor. Just as the tabernacle had been His idea, the construction of the temple would also be done at His initiative, not at that of any man. When God would fill the temple with His glory, the people could have every confidence that their God was present among them (see 1 Kings 8:10–11).

In the generations from the Exodus until David's rule, Yahweh had never demanded a permanent place to dwell. Unlike the pagan gods, He didn't *need* a place to dwell. His plans for a house would correlate with the rest He had promised to give the people. God's resting presence would be their resting peace if they trusted Him in obedience. He assured David that the plans for a temple would be carried out when Solomon took the throne.

David's son Solomon wasted no time beginning the temple work once his kingship was secured. Positioned on Mount Moriah in Jerusalem, the house of the Lord was built of the finest materials and employed tens of thousands of people during the seven years of its construction. Early on, the Lord made a very clear, conditional promise to Solomon:

> As for this temple you are building—if you walk in My statutes, observe My ordinances, and keep all My commands by walking in them, I will fulfill My promise to you, which I made to your father David. *I will live among the Israelites and not abandon My people Israel.* (1 Kings 6:12–13)

Following Solomon's dedication of the completed temple, the Lord responded with His promise to be with the people. "I have consecrated this temple you have built, to put My name there forever; *My eyes and My heart will be there at all times*" (1 Kings 9:3).

More promises of His presence! Was there anything else

that Israel needed? Could there be any desire that His presence among His people would leave unmet? Everything that they needed would fall under the umbrella of His sovereign, governing presence. Everything that *we* need falls under the umbrella of His sovereign, governing presence.

Think about it. Is there a desire in your heart that the Lord's nearness cannot meet? Loneliness, longing, pain, need—He is the answer to every ache. He is the Friend to the lonely. He is the Father to the fatherless. Though a womb may be empty, the Lord can fill the heart with joy. With steadfast love He gives reserves of perseverance when our bodies are broken and painful. The Lord provides in times of need, but our position of dependence on Him for every need requires a deep, sweet relationship of trust. Remember—desperation isn't the worst thing that can happen to us. Desperation and neediness keep us near His side. This is where we most need to be.

I'm familiar with loneliness, infertility, physical pain, financial need. Each time my needs have risen to the surface, the Lord has answered my prayers with His presence. Sometimes I have welcomed Him, and sometimes I have rejected Him for another "fix" —but His presence has always been the answer.

## Prophets, Priests, and Kings

Though he is often considered a good king, King Solomon was a confusing composite of wisdom, success, and lust. Though he sought the Lord at times and was blessed with wisdom directly from God, his heart yearned for physical satiation—or so he thought. He kept hundreds of women who turned his heart away from Yahweh. His rampant sexual sin led to rampant idolatry, and the kingdom suffered as a result. Solomon had a divided heart, and his countrymen weren't much different. Israel found a misplaced comfort in the temple itself, not in God's presence in it. As long as the temple stood firm, they thought they could live how they wanted and expect success as a kingdom. Their faith was anchored to the place, not to the God who dwelled there. Complacency reigned in Israel. God was in the temple, so they could live as they pleased, right? Wrong. Confidence in God's presence should never give us license to take Him for granted. He is still a holy God.

Solomon's son Rehoboam ultimately split the kingdom because of his foolish and hard-hearted dealings with the people. They rebelled, and the kingdom was divided into two separate entities. Rehoboam took the southern kingdom, which consisted of only the cities in Judah, including Jerusalem. A man called Jeroboam (the similarity of the names makes this confusing!) won over the rest of God's people in Israel, the northern kingdom, by setting up two golden calves and many shrines nearby for worship. He instituted new festivals to mimic the ones in Judah and changed the calendar so the people wouldn't be tempted to return to Jerusalem. Jeroboam allowed anyone who desired it to act as priest. This perversion of God's law made a mockery of the way He had chosen to dwell among His people. The proper, ordained ways of worshiping God were desecrated, and for this reason the northern kingdom soon came to a decisive and destructive end.

The ratio of good kings to bad kings throughout the rest of Judah's history is dismal. Only a few moments brighten what is mostly a dark, discouraging path to exile. In kindness and mercy, God spoke through prophets to warn the people that their sin would result in separation from Him. Through Isaiah, Jeremiah, Micah, Amos, and many more, the Lord repeatedly gave detailed messages about what would happen if Judah continued down the path toward wickedness. The prophets warned God's people about their lack of true affection for Yahweh, and yet the kingdom of Judah moved forward with little regard for loyalty, worship, or justice. God gave them years and years to repent, but they refused to turn their hearts to Him when their creature comforts were supplied by whatever delighted their idolatrous hearts.

God followed through with His warnings. Jerusalem was destroyed by the pagan Babylonians. As judgment, God removed His presence from the temple, as the prophet Ezekiel had promised: "Then the glory of the LORD went out from the threshold of the house, and stood over the cherubim" (Ezek. 10:18 ESV). When He removed His glory from the temple, the people and their city were open to attack from their enemies. The temple that Judah so confidently trusted for protection was razed. The people of God may have now felt physically exiled from His protective presence, but in truth their hearts had abandoned Him long ago. In mercy, God allowed a remnant of His people to be taken captive and sent to Babylon for seventy years.

The destruction of Judah and the subsequent exile shouldn't have surprised anyone—God had given ample warning through the prophets and many opportunities for repentance. The people, however, continued their pattern of unbelief and half-hearted worship. Though their resistance to God's sobering prophecies is mind-boggling to anyone who reads through their sordid history, I see that same bent toward self-gratification in my own heart.

Though this was a dark period of history, God wasn't losing control. Even as he allowed the consequences for idolatry to roll out, He still planned to pull an eternal King from the line of David and the people of Judah. We should be astounded by God's unending patience with our slowness to repent. Though He allows suffering—whether as consequence or as refining— He doesn't do it to be cruel. He was not arbitrary in the exile of His people. He's not arbitrary in whatever form of suffering you are currently experiencing. Whatever He allows in our lives is meant, in every way, to draw us back to Him. I can see Him doing that in every dark day of my own life.

## If Nothing Changes, Is He Still Enough?

Two years into my growing relationship with unexplained physical pain, our adoption process abruptly ended when the country closed its program. Knowing that there were millions of orphans in that one small country but finding ourselves unable to help even one, we grieved the loss of the child we had hoped to adopt as well as the nearly three years we'd invested in the process.

Our social worker reconstructed our home study and paperwork as quickly as possible so we could move to domestic adoption without delay. We rushed to complete the new paperwork and to schedule home visits; we went for our fourth trip to be fingerprinted and requested yet another round of background checks. I spent hours creating a book of pictures and information to detail our life as a family in hopes that a prospective mother might consider us for her child. We finished everything in record time. We waited.

*This time it will work,* I told myself. *This time we won't have to wait, and I'll finally be happy.* I knew better—but I wanted to believe that having another child would end my yearning to grow our family. Sure, God was with me—but if He answered this one specific prayer, *then* I could believe that He is enough. It would help me to cope with the other problems in my life. But the trouble is that it was never just *one specific prayer.*

Days went by, then weeks and months. Every once in a while, an email would pop up with the words "I'm sorry, but another family has been chosen . . ." I lay in bed at night working through the reasons we had been rejected. It was such a familiar feeling. Our floundering local church ministry had schooled me in rejection, but experiencing it on multiple levels made us feel like we were missing something or doing something wrong. My husband and I took turns sitting on the couch in the dark with a hundred questions for the Lord. Adoption? Church ministry? Physical pain? God was silent during those long nights. We waited for anything to change.

The desire for another child made my heart ache, the silent disease made my body ache, but the fractured relationship I had with my church made my soul ache. My affection for the body of Christ was bruised at best, but my desire was for her good. I knew that Jesus was committed to her—but I wasn't sure that I could be.

My journals during those years of ministry turmoil are filled with conversations—some of them hard to believe. I wrote down every act of betrayal, every false accusation. I couldn't talk to anyone about what I knew; there was no refuge for the pastor's wife. So I wrote it down in incriminating detail. I needed to see that we were not crazy—that things really were spinning out of control—and I wanted to purge the angry thoughts and feelings that were roiling inside. I'm plagued with a mind that can recall a conversation, word for word, years after the fact. I used that gift to outline my grievances—to justify my dissipating affection for the church. Some entries are a desperate fight for hope; others are depositions of defense. It's ugly—all of it. Every word is a memory I'd like to erase. But I wrote it in ink, and I remember it indelibly.

Our ministry troubles in that small town have had a far-reaching influence that we are still struggling to overcome years later. Watching our church family repeatedly splinter apart has had long-term effects on my feelings about the bride of Christ—and, I've since discovered, has had similar effects on my church family as well. That familiar coping mechanism of walling myself in has been one of the greatest temptations of my adulthood. Vulnerability in front of the people who had the greatest capacity to hurt me seemed too risky.

For years, I vacillated regularly between love and disdain for the church. I thought it was just the bad hand we'd been dealt. I had no idea that my relationship with the church was a pivotal means by which the Lord would teach me to treasure His presence.

If you see yourself in my resolve to avoid close relationships in the church, please stay with me. If you're still recovering from wounds inflicted by people in your church past, please don't stop reading. The Lord can do strange, marvelous things with your pain. He can teach you to love His bride. I would have bristled at words like these back then—but they are the words I needed to hear and wish now that someone had said to me.

Whether I was walking the floors of my home in the dark out of despair over ministry or over our lengthening adoption process or out of fear that I'd never find relief from pain, the same questions rolled around in my head. If the doors of my desires remained closed, was God still enough for me? If He never opened them, was He still with me? If our ministry never recovered, was God still with us? If we never had another child, was He still good to us? If He never healed me from the physical pain that was beginning to shape my days, was He still faithfully loving me?

I didn't know for certain. Generally speaking, I knew that God was good because Scripture says that He is. I wasn't so sure about His love and kindness to *me* specifically, though. I thought that perhaps He loved me in the way that you love a relative who's kind of annoying but is still family, and so you *have* to love them. I'd certainly logged enough complaints to Him to merit that kind of begrudging love.

I asked Him my questions, but He was quiet. Does silence mean absence? Was He still with me? I worried that the silence I observed from Him would stretch out like the blank space between the Old and New Testaments. Is God still with us when He quietly asks us to wait?

## Does Silence Mean Absence?

The small remnant of God's people who survived Judah's destruction spent a lifetime in exile in Babylon. Neither visitors nor citizens, they lived an odd existence away from their home-land. They trusted God in their exile, though. It's funny how a loss of freedom cultivates dependence on God. "Even in our slav-ery, God has given us new life and light to our eyes. Though we are slaves, our God has not abandoned us in our slavery" (Ezra 9:8–9).

When the Persian king finally sent them back home, God's people felt an urgency to rebuild the temple and reinstate the rhythms of worship. Again, the idea of the temple structure made them feel secure. Under the leadership of Ezra and then Nehemiah, they rebuilt Jerusalem's broken walls. Though they were free to worship and live their lives as the people of God, they were never really free from the rule of foreign nations again. They rebuilt their city walls and temple under a watchful Persian eye. Though the reading of the law in   generated an excitement among the people to follow Yahweh again, the stresses of living under foreign rule in their own land led to a waning of their loyalty. Their worship of the Lord lacked genuine affection.

The final prophets warned the people about their indifference toward Yahweh. Their paucity of genuine worship revealed itself in poor versions of worship (as they brought maimed, less-than-perfect animals for sacrifice), direct disobedience to the Lord (as they intermarried with foreign nations the Lord had prohibited in order to protect them from idolatry), withholding tithes (which revealed their greed and lack of trust in God's provision), and injustice toward one another. Israel was not living as the set-apart people of God. True worship stems from the heart, but they were robbing God of the glory that was due Him.

Like every prophet before him, Malachi warned of impend-ing judgment if nothing changed but offered hope if the people would submit themselves to God's warning. "For indeed, the day is coming, burning like a furnace, when all the arrogant and every-one who commits wickedness will become stubble. The coming day will consume them . . . not leaving them root or branches. But for you who fear My name, the sun of righteousness will rise with healing in its wings, and you will go out and playfully jump like calves from the stall" (Mal. 4:1–2).

The last recorded words of this last Old Testament prophet promised the coming of Elijah, one of Israel's great, long-gone prophets, in anticipation of the coming day of the Lord. "And he will turn the hearts of fathers to their children and the hearts of children to their fathers" (Mal. 4:6).

What followed were four hundred silent years. It's a blank page, maybe two, in our Bibles. But it was *four hundred years*. There were no more words from the Lord who had long spoken to His people through prophets, judges, and kings. No more promises were made. No more obvious manifestations of God's presence hovered in the temple. There was just the question of whether God would keep the promises He had already made.

I wonder what it was like to live during those quiet years—to know your long history of God's manifest presence and to live in the hope that He would be faithful to keep His word. I wonder if the generations of Israelites knew what they were waiting for. During those four hundred years, the rule of foreign nations made way for the tyranny of Roman rule and the oppression of the people of God. Oppression led to desperation. By the time the New Testament opens, the people are living under extreme financial strain beneath the excessive taxation of Rome. Surely they cried out for the Lord's deliverance. Once again, they were a people waiting for the Lord to end their suffering. (Doesn't that sound familiar?)

The entire situation raises some key questions: Had God abandoned His people? Though silent, was He present? Had He completely removed His presence from them once Solomon's temple was destroyed? Does God's silence mean absence?

It is His nature to be present, everywhere at once—to be

omnipresent. Even if His special, recognized presence was absent, it was not His nature to be absent from the people whom He loved and had set His name on. The Lord was silent during those centuries in fulfillment of prophecy: "Hear this! The days are coming—this is the declaration of the Lord GOD—when I will send a famine . . . of hearing the words of the LORD" (Amos 8:11). Though silence was a consequence of Israel's rebellion, it seems that God was also preparing His people to understand presence differently from how they had thus far. He was moving from living among His people corporately to living as one of them physically to eventually dwelling in them (and in us) individually.

The removal of His glory from among the people of Israel wasn't all bad news. God would not be contained in a building on a mountain to be worshiped by just one kind of people anymore. At the end of the four hundred years, everything would change about the way God's people understood His presence and how they approached Him. Actually, absolutely everything on earth would change, period. God's flesh-and-blood presence would split history in two.

God's silence doesn't indicate that He is absent. As we will examine more in chapter 8, we have direct access to God because we have the gift of His Spirit. If we have believed that Jesus has paid for our sins at the cross, and if God has made us alive in Christ, then we can be certain that He will never leave us. If He has given us new hearts that long to be satisfied by Him only, then we can take confidence in the fact that He will keep His promise to be with us. He has grafted us into His family.

Even when we struggle with His silence, He keeps His promises. He is still present when He asks us to wait. He might be using silence to teach us to hold fast to Him—to exercise what faith really is: believing when you can't see. Trusting that He is there when you aren't sure what's next. He doesn't abandon us when we experience suffering or even when we bear the consequences for our sin. The coming of Jesus changed the way in which God would be with His people, and because of this, you and I can have confidence that He is enough for us. Even in silence. Even in waiting.

## Discussion Questions

1. When we feel that God is silent regarding our circumstances, we frequently default to doubting His faithfulness. Why do you think doubt is often our first response?

2. What might we be missing about God's character when we equate His goodness with only good circumstances?

3. Do you struggle to believe that that God is good to *you* specifically? List some Scriptures you can call to mind when you are tempted to doubt His love for you. (Here are a few to get you started: Romans 5:8; Ephesians 3:14–19; 1 John 4:9–11.)

4. After generations of idolatry and rebellion, the kingdoms of Israel and Judah were destroyed, leaving only a small remnant of people who were taken captive and exiled for seventy years to a foreign country. How was God being good to His people when He sent judgment for their continued disobedience? *Was* He being good to them? yes

5. Share your thoughts about the long period of silence at the end of the Old Testament. Was God communicating that He was absent from His people during His silence? yes

See page - 90

# Part 2

What We Gained
at the Cross

# 6

# O Come, O Come, Emmanuel

*For every look at yourself, take ten looks at Christ. . . . Let
your soul be filled with a heart-ravishing sense of the sweetness
and excellency of Christ and all that is in Him . . . so there
will be no room for folly, or the world, or Satan, or the flesh.*

—Robert Murray McCheyne

Before Genesis, He was. Before the garden, before the fruit and
the snake and the shame, He was. Before the Lord spoke words
that formed stars and dirt from nothing, tree branches and blades
of grass from emptiness, He was. Before there was light, He was.
Jesus was.

Jesus, the Son, was with God in the beginning, existing perfectly, needing nothing. And then, in a moment, He wasn't. In one
strategic, history-splitting moment, He wasn't existing perfectly
at the Father's side; He wasn't self-sufficient or in control of the
universe the way He had been. He became, in a fractured instant,
an embryo carried inside a young, unmarried Jewish woman in a
poor village in Israel.

Let the gravity of it fall on you: a King in heaven, and then a
fetus. The presence of God in the form of an unborn baby. It feels
wrong. It seems out of character. In the past, standing too near the

ground on which the Lord's presence rested would strike a man dead; but now the Son of God slept in a teenager's belly, sucking His thumb and dreaming the dreams of the unborn. His whole world was wrapped in amniotic fluid; His only responsibilities were the work of growing fingernails and eyelashes. Tethered to His mother's body, the one through whom all things were created was helplessly tied to the business of being human.

God had heard the cry of His people during those many silent years. He'd removed His corporately known, manifest presence from among them—but He hadn't abandoned them. He had listened and waited until the time was right. He could have done anything—could have come at any point in any manner that would inspire respect and demand fealty from the people of Israel. It's what they were expecting, anyway—a king like great King David of generations past. God's promise to David in 2 Samuel 7 was of a family line that would produce a king, so the people were looking for someone with power. A political leader, maybe, or a hero with a vast army and endless resources. Anything that would assert power and dominion and would pull the people from beneath the heel of Rome. They had waited four hundred years, after all. The last time they had waited so long for rescue, Moses had showed up with plagues and deliverance and a sea that was split open for a miraculous crossing. The next deliverer would come like that, right?

Well, no. Not exactly.

Jesus came helpless and needy, the way *we* come—helpless and needy. A baby needs everything. It takes months for a baby to even realize that he has *hands*, let alone to know how to use those hands to feed or dress himself. Babies are at the mercy of the ones who provide for them. And this helplessness is the robe that heaven's King chose to wear. Wrapped in swaddling blankets and an infant's frailty, the One who was with Yahweh for eternity backward, the One through whom God created every molecule, the One who was always with His heavenly Father—Jesus made His debut in an unwedded pregnancy followed by a rural barn delivery.

From the eternal Prince to a newborn baby. From heaven's throne to a feeding trough. From scepter to slobbering. The Agent of Creation was a baby who didn't even know He had hands yet. Why did He do it this way? God's people weren't expecting this.

And it would be just like them to decide that God's chosen means of being present with His people was not enough for them. Angels may have sung when the Prince of heaven was born in Bethlehem's dirty stable, but this baby would become familiar with a song of dissatisfaction. He would be the first to completely reject the tune. Though He had every right, by our standards, to be discontent with His earthly life, He sang a different song, spoke a different word, and wore human skin better than we ever could.

People would sing the song to Him, though. They would reject Him, mock Him, ignore Him, hate Him, use Him, betray Him. He would prove that the way God had planned to be with His people was the best way. In order for him to show them that their longings were for the One who had made them, there was just one way for him to dwell among His people: He had to *become* one of them.

## What Were You Expecting?

The people weren't looking for this baby Savior to be born to a poor carpenter's family. All they knew of Yahweh was smoke and tents, clouds and temples. The stories they passed down were full of fire and fury, rent seas and perplexing plagues. The God whom they knew was big and loud and fearsome. At least, that's what they thought. Could He really rescue them in such a humble manner?

If they'd been listening, really listening, they would have heard the whispers of the coming infant King. The prophets had spoken of the coming Rescuer. Isaiah had called him a Servant, not a political potentate. A servant. He'd talked about how undesirable He would be. A few saw Him coming: Zechariah, Elizabeth, Mary, Joseph, an old priest, an ancient prophetess, some foreign star-followers.

But that's it. Corporately, there was no search for a Suffering Servant or a baby who would be born in a barn. If they'd been looking closely for Yahweh, they would have seen His Son. Their mistake was not that they didn't look but that they looked for the wrong person. God has always chosen the ways in which He will keep His promise of presence, but we tend to see what we want to see. We'll call Him good if He answers our prayers within the exact perimeters that we give Him, but God is good to us even when His answer looks wildly different from what we expect. Or even when His answer seems like no answer at all.

He does things in ways that seem backward to us. If we can look at Him instead of the distractions of our circumstances, we might be able to see Him being good to us in ways that we don't expect. We might question what we know of Him. And if our questions send us to the Word so that we truly see this God who is good to us in unexpected ways, then the questions are well worth asking.

## O Come, O Come, Emmanuel, to This Old Couch

I thought I knew Him. I mean, I did know Him.

I'd been fed with the gospel from infancy. I'd walked with God closely as a child, passionately through my teenage years, distantly as a young adult. But now, as a grown woman, I found myself hungering after Him—the one constant presence in my life. But new, difficult circumstances made me question what I knew of Him—this one who had been silent while my faith leaked with fear. My life was a sieve of doubt. Yet where else could I go? It had to be Him.

"God is good—all the time!" This joyfully proclaimed platitude was my only exposure to responsive readings during my church experience, and as ingrained as it was in the liturgy of my Baptist upbringing, I struggled to believe it when suffering characterized my days. The truest thing in my life pulled too tight, making it hard to breathe and harder to remember. I was wrapped up in one single word: pain.

My early mornings on my old, beige couch had begun to look different. In our early days of ministry trouble, I had desperately combed the Word. Later, I had sulked through my second period of waiting for a child with an open Bible and a dry heart, due to force of habit and tiny hints of hope. Now, I sat with a mass of pillows, packs of ice and heat, and a hollow-eyed hunger for the Lord to rescue me from the fiery pull of physical pain.

The slow burn that crept up my spine in the mornings turned into an inferno that surged through my hips and back with alarming intensity every single night. Sleep was elusive—a commodity I would have paid for if I could have found the right currency. Each night I was shaken from sleep by breath-stealing pain. It ran up and down my vertebrae, settling in the space above my hips and causing the muscles to spasm involuntarily.

Night was hard, and it took all morning to recover. Stiff and sore, I'd sip coffee at dawn, pretending I'd meant to be up that early. Truthfully, I was regularly awake and in agony by 2:30 a.m. The persistence of the pain gnawed at my sanity. In the mornings, I tried to sort it out. I would open my Bible and make two columns in my head. Here's what's true; here's what's not. Pain is true; God is true. But pain is also a liar that tells me that God isn't true, or that if He is true He definitely isn't good, or that if He is good He definitely isn't good to me. I would pick at that frayed strand of thought until the sun came up.

Separating truth from fiction was important, I knew. My Bible was heavy with words that I knew would help me to put things in the proper "true" and "not true" columns, but I didn't know where to start. Same couch, same Bible, same chipped coffee mug—different brand of desperation that rose with the sun. That old dry-spell habit was there from muscle memory, and I was desperate again. I wanted to know that God hadn't abandoned me—needed to know that there would be an end to this pain. Like always, I opened up the ancient words of God to see what was in them for me, what would help me, what would encourage me. It had worked in the past; it had to work now.

But, clenched in the grip of pain and fear, I felt that this search-and-find approach to Scripture was failing me. It wasn't enough. I was afraid that everything I'd ever believed about the Lord was built on the false premise that God's love equaled comfort and ease. Was He suddenly different? Had He changed in His silence? Had I?

Pain *had* changed me. It made me jittery, fearful. It made me question myself. It woke me nightly to remind me of its faithfulness. It would never leave me or forsake me. While I paced the floor, I wondered if God loved me. While I alternated between heat and ice, I wondered if He saw me. When I threw the empty bottle of Tylenol in the trash, I wondered if He noticed. When my hair began to fall out and my skin erupted in scaly rashes, I questioned His goodness. When the circles beneath my eyes hollowed out, when I dropped twenty pounds, when my head was so foggy with cobwebbed confusion that I questioned my ability to drive across town to the store, I asked what the Lord was doing to me.

Night after night, the presence of pain edged out my belief in the presence of God. I couldn't understand why He would allow it. Was He punishing me? Teaching me? Treating me like an unloved stepchild? Was He killing some sin in me? Or was He just killing me?

We pray for deliverance when suffering steals our days and nights, and we *should* pray to that end. But we must do so with the knowledge that we need the Deliverer more than we need deliverance. When we don't understand why the One who can heal us won't, we must turn our hearts to Him anyway. Who else has the words of life? Suffering may be the tool He uses to pin us to His side by sending us to the Word. But instead of looking for ourselves in the Scriptures—for what they might reveal about our potential deliverance—we should fix our gaze on God, from whom deliverance flows.

I had always looked for myself in the Word, but I needed a new approach. I couldn't trust myself to separate fact from fiction. I needed help in order to see what was true. Was pain a liar? Or was God? Was He still good when He didn't alleviate my suffering? I was afraid of what I would find.

### It's Him We Need

I began in the book of Isaiah. Admittedly, it was an unusual place to start. Isaiah brims with dismal prophecies about Israel's doomed future if they continued to disobey Yahweh, and Israel's resistance to repentance meant that those dismal prophecies were carried out. However, I remembered all the big statements about God in chapter 40 and the descriptions of the coming Messiah in chapter 53, and these seemed promising for my experiment.

I had humble tools: a spiral notebook, a pen, and a lot of desperation. These are tools you probably have in your arsenal right now. The thing about fixing your gaze on God is that it doesn't take much beyond a spirit that is willing to do it. God has given us Himself through His Word. In Him we have everything we need! Here's how I used my simple tools: every time the prophet made a statement about God, I wrote it down. Whatever Scripture said, I wrote it down. It was the first time in all my life as a believer that

I had examined the text exclusively for what it would teach me about God.

I didn't know what I was looking for exactly, and I was surprised by what I found. Pen in hand, I scribbled out statements about Yahweh, about the coming Suffering Servant whom we know as Jesus, about the Spirit who would rest on the people of God. As the burning pain of night melted into the stiffness of morning, I could be found on the couch trying to quiet my pain by fixating on the character of God. Morning by morning, new mercies I saw.

Turning my eyes to the Lord was difficult at first. I was so used to looking for a cure for what ailed me. But, as the days rolled into weeks and months, opening the worn pages of my Bible and looking at God became reflexive.

Slowly, without my realizing it, my life separated into two categories: before and after. Not before and after my deferred hopes were fulfilled, but before and after God's presence became more important to me than those deferred hopes were. Everything changed when my focal point moved from myself to my Creator. Gazing on the character of God, I beheld His presence in the middle of my suffering, right in the middle of my living room. It didn't end my suffering. Looking at Him instead of at myself helped me to persevere through it. Jen Wilkin explains it well: "Our insecurities, fears, and doubts can never be banished by the knowledge of who we are. They can only be banished by the knowledge of 'I AM.'"[1] The shift in my thinking came as the result of my gazing at the character of God. Scripture revealed that He was with me—that the gift was His presence, not necessarily the removal of pain.

What we need more than physical or emotional healing is the Healer Himself. We think that we're looking for one kind of

---

1. Jen Wilkin, *Women of the Word: How to Study the Bible with Both Our Hearts and Our Minds* (Wheaton, IL: Crossway, 2014), 26.

answer to our prayer when it's the One whom we pray to that we need the most. Searching for Him in the Scriptures brings restoration to our hearts. Resting our eyes on His goodness seals up cracks of doubt. Knowing God as He has revealed Himself in Scripture bolsters our faith. It's how we know He is with us—and He is enough.

Though I wanted to be healed from physical pain, the words of Isaiah 19 revealed to me that God is purposeful with the pain that He allows into our lives.

> When they cry out to the LORD because of their oppressors, He will send them a savior and leader, and he will rescue them. The LORD will make Himself known to Egypt, and Egypt will know the LORD on that day. They will offer sacrifices and offerings; they will make vows to the LORD and fulfill them. The LORD will strike Egypt, striking and healing. Then they will return to the LORD and He will hear their prayers and heal them. (Isa. 19:20–22)

My pain felt like judgment, but sometimes God permits suffering in order to grab our hearts. He draws us to His Word so that we will know Him. So that we will follow Him closely. So that we will not run after our other desires.

While pain and suffering result from the fall, it is not beyond the reach of God to use them for good. Pain can provide the right posture for us to look up and see God as the one who answers every ache and yearning. Dwelling on His character allows us to enjoy His very near presence. To see Him in His Word is to know that He is with you and to enjoy His presence. Even in pain. Especially in pain.

Watching my friends grow their families effortlessly stirred up bitterness in my heart. Yet Scripture's reminder of God's sovereignty brought me quiet rebuke. "God is the Creator of the heavens. He formed the earth and made it. He established it; He did not create it to be empty, but formed it to be inhabited—'I am Yahweh, and there is no other. I have not spoken in secret, somewhere in a land of darkness. I did not say to the descendants of Jacob: Seek Me in a wasteland. I, Yahweh, speak truthfully; I say what is right'" (Isa. 45:18–19).

In the past, I would have studied the words in my Bible for a possible extra meaning, but this approach isn't just selfish but also unnecessary. Feeding the soul with sustenance grown from God's immutable character is enough. It is more than enough to sustain us when we grieve, hurt, fight, worry, wonder, hope, or fear. He is more than enough. We do not need "extra" or "deeper" meanings beyond Scripture. God doesn't expect us to unearth some new truth that's particular to our own situation in order to get what we need from the Word. The Word as He has given it to us is what we need. Taking Him at this word is more than enough.

## A Big Goodness

My circumstances did not change. And I am glad—for changed circumstances would have been the hero of my story. God would have been good only in the sense that He had released me from pain. I wouldn't have known that He can be kind to us in the middle of the pain. No, my circumstances remained the same. In the crucible of pain, I learned that the Lord's goodness transcends suffering. It breaks through sorrow, for it is bigger than sorrow.

As I combed through the pages of Isaiah, the words of the prophet painted a picture of God's character that eclipsed my small view of His goodness. "I will make known the LORD's faithful love and the LORD's praiseworthy acts, because of all the LORD has done for us—even the many good things He has done for the house of Israel and has done for them based on His compassion and the abundance of His faithful love" (Isa. 63:7). God's goodness is tied to His character, and His divine attributes are not diminished by our poor understanding of them.

When we make the mistake of equating God's inherent goodness with what seems good to us, we limit our belief in His ability to be good. But He is good in all things—even in suffering, even in pain. His goodness is limitless; it cannot be confined to the days when our lives work out in the ways that we hope. That's a small, tight perimeter for God's goodness.

My grandmother is known for correcting people on their finite views of God's goodness. When the doctor's report is good, when we escape a car accident, when we have just enough money for the utility bill, we are quick to say, "God is good!" My ninety-two-year-old grandmother always points out that God would still be good if the report had been bad, if we had wrecked the car, if the bill hadn't been paid on time. He would still be good, because *it is His nature to be good.*

> I am Yahweh, and there is no other;
> there is no God but Me.
> I will strengthen you,
> though you do not know Me,
> so that all may know from the rising of the sun to its setting
> that there is no one but Me.
> I am Yahweh, and there is no other. (Isa. 45:5–6).

Even when we're not aware of His goodness, He still maintains it.

Goodness that is limited to comfortable circumstances is a small goodness. But goodness that permeates even our darkest nights, goodness that is present in our most piercing moments of pain, goodness that lifts our weary chins and comforts us with its presence—that is a big goodness, a goodness that lasts, a goodness that does not turn with shadows or fade with change. That is God's goodness. His goodness alone can transcend our sorrows, because He does not change. God's goodness is a fixed point among the rotations and revolutions of our sufferings and longings. Like the Savior in the manger, this goodness is unexpected—but it is what we need.

"'Though the mountains move and the hills shake, My love will not be removed from you and My covenant of peace will not be shaken,' says your compassionate LORD" (Isa. 54:10). The Lord's chosen method of goodness is its best possible manifestation. And there is joy in it. "Therefore the LORD is waiting to show you mercy, and is rising up to show you compassion, for the LORD is a just God. All who wait patiently for Him are happy" (Isa. 30:18).

Turning my face to Him on the dark nights that were saturated with pain was the kindest thing He could have done for me. If He had healed me first, relief would have been my treasure— when instead I needed to see that *He* is the treasure. He is faithful to give us what we need the most, and that will always be His presence. If you're in a period of suffering now, there's nothing wrong with praying for God to bring it to an end. But don't miss what He might be teaching you in the meantime. Sorrow and suffering can be catalysts for us to see God's transcendent goodness. When suffering has emptied us of all the fleeting comforts of earth, we finally see that all we have is Christ. And it is then that we know that Christ is all we need.

As the waiting Israelites did, we need the nearness of God more than anything else. More than healing, more than children, more than changed circumstances, more than resolution . . . we need Christ. Jesus is the expression of God's nearness that His people didn't know they were waiting for but have always needed.

## The Christ We've Always Needed

Everyone who has been born after Jesus has had the privilege of looking at the Old Testament with Him in their peripheral vision. We can find His name on every page of our Bibles—if not directly, then in the way that earth and all humanity longs, yearns, buckles under their hunger for a reconciliation that only Jesus could provide.

But there *are* direct mentions of His name. Micah and Isaiah and Zechariah all spoke of the coming One—a King, a Prince, a baby, a child, a Servant of Suffering, a Shepherd. He would be an amalgam of humble and high, suffering and supreme, gentle and judging. In their longing for a deliverer who would pull them from Rome's iron fist, Israel lost sight of the prophesies of His humility, suffering, and gentleness. They looked for what they thought they needed most: a powerful earthly king who would vanquish their enemies.

God had much farther-reaching plans for the birth of the infant Son. He would send them a King to deliver them—along with all who would believe—from the shackles of sin, Satan, and death. He was sending them what they needed most: His presence. He would do it up close. He would do it in person. He would do it while wearing human skin—while experiencing every form of rejection and betrayal. In a small town, in a small birth, came a small human who carried the weight of heaven and earth on his shoulders. In the fragility of a newborn baby lay the hope of us all. Joseph's mingled-together fear and courage, Mary's blood on the ground—it must have felt like hope. Born in a bath of water and blood, the One with no beginning began His earthly kingdom among the lowing of cows and sheep.

Immanuel—*God with us.* Jesus was the fullest, most tangible expression of God's presence the earth had ever known. God's eternal Son was breathing the same oxygen as the ones He had created. He was held in the arms of parents He had created. The Ancient of Days, the one without beginning, the agent of all creation, became a new life that took a first breath and felt human helplessness. This is the mystery and the miracle of the incarnation: the One who made us became one of us, in order to save us.

## A Tent, a Man, and a God
## Who Keeps His Promises

Back in the desert, back in the wandering, back in the history of God's early demonstrations of His promised presence, He lived in a tent, a tabernacle, among His people. Remember? God's glory came down with the unmistakable presence of a thick smoke. There was no missing it.

Thousands of years later, when one of Jesus's dearest friends penned the words to his gospel, this word *tabernacle* showed up again. John said of Jesus's coming, "The Word became flesh and took up residence among us. We observed His glory, the glory as the One and Only Son from the Father, full of grace and truth" (John 1:14). John used the Greek word for "tabernacle," *skenoo*, as a verb. Jesus *tabernacled* among us when He "took up residence."

God's promises are woven together seamlessly throughout history as proof that He will be with His people. He promised Abraham, Isaac, Jacob, Judah, and David that He would be with them, and He continued to keep that promise in ways they couldn't have imagined. Just as He pitched a tent in the desert of Israel's consequences, He pitched a tent of human skin and tabernacled among His people in order to keep the promise of His presence. For years it was a voice, a cloud, a fire, some smoke . . . and then silence. It was always Him—but suddenly, breaking history into before and after, it was *Him with us*. It was Him as one of us.

The people weren't looking for Him in the right way, because we seldom look for anything in the way God wants us to. We didn't expect to find a King in a barn. We weren't looking for the Creator of the universe to put on skin and bones. We were surprised by royalty putting on frailty. We didn't imagine that we would get

God *with* us—but we needed God with us. We needed Immanuel. And this changed everything about how people would know God's nearness.

You and I didn't get to meet Jesus on earth, of course. But that doesn't mean we don't benefit from His coming. We stand to gain everything from it! In our longings to be healed, loved, filled, and seen, we find everything that we need in Christ. Even if the specific things that we pray for are met with what seems like silence, it may be that God is urging us to look at Him as the answer to our prayers. We miss the Giver when we focus solely on the gifts. Even in our suffering, Jesus is the one we will always need. Our hearts will always hunger for Him.

### Discussion Questions

1. Familiarity with the story of the birth of Jesus can cause us to tune out and miss the miracle of the incarnation. Take a moment to reflect on Colossians 1:15–23, and list the ways that Christ's coming was not what we expected but was exactly what we needed.

2. Jesus tells us in John 17:17 that God's word is truth. When our circumstances make it difficult for us to distinguish truth from lies, what practices can help us to determine what's true about God?

3. Have you made a habit of studying Scripture with a "what's in it for me" approach? How might reframing your question and asking "What do I learn about God?" change the way that you understand the Bible?

4. "Scripture revealed that He was with me—that the gift was His presence, not necessarily the removal of pain." Is God enough for you if He doesn't change your circumstances for "the better"? How can we press through unchanged circumstances with a certainty of God's sufficiency?

5. In light of the Old Testament manifestations of God's presence, explain the significance of John's use of the word "tabernacled" in regard to Jesus's coming and living among us (see John 1:14).

# 7

# Never Alone

*When we see Jesus, we see the glory of God
as in no other manifestation.*

—JOHN PIPER

Wrapped in swaddling clothes, running and playing with other children, learning the trade of carpentry—Jesus's humanity meant that God could be touched by human hands. He could be jostled in a crowd, clapped on the back in a hearty greeting, kissed on the cheek by His mother. People saw the skin crinkle around his eyes when He laughed, smelled His sweat when they stood close to Him. Jesus, full of humanity and divinity, was a walking, holy composite of Maker and made—one hundred percent God, one hundred percent man. The baby in the manger grew into a man, and though Scripture gives us little detail about His growing-up years, we do know that He was strong, full of wisdom, and covered in God's grace.

In the gospels, thirty-year-old Jesus emerges full of truth and grit and confidence. He knew who He was, and He wielded that knowledge well. He wasn't just an emissary or representative of God's presence. He was God, present. He was still Immanuel.

Rather than boasting in His kingship, Jesus washed feet. Rather than demanding worship, He wrapped Himself in quiet and soli-tude to pray to His Father. Rather than gathering a loyal army, Jesus called together an unlikely bunch of hot-headed, loud-mouthed, uneducated fisherman and a few unlikely former sinners. Rather than demanding a palace, He roamed the countryside as an itiner-ant preacher. Rather than fighting for fame, He slipped away from crowds and urged people to keep quiet about His identity. Rather than strolling up to Caesar to take a throne that He deserved, He paid His taxes and submitted to the governing authorities.

He wasn't uncomfortable with the diseases of those who begged to be healed. He rebuked sin while also forgiving it. He touched festering wounds and sightless eyes. He addressed broken hearts and minds that were bound by the enemy. He spoke truth with fierce conviction that was tempered by deep compassion. No one could wear the weight of humanity and deity like Jesus.

## Just Come

When the presence of God traveled the Judean countryside preaching the good news of the kingdom of heaven, the fulfill-ment of numerous Old Testament prophecies rested on His shoulders. Time is rightly divided into everything before and everything after His life on earth. Jesus was the answer to history's long yearning for redemption. He was the fullest display of God's promise to dwell with His people—the most tangible version of it to date. Yet there was a mixed reaction to His presence.

People begged for more miracles, displaying (as always) the desire to be satisfied by something other than the One who per-forms the signs and wonders. During His three years of teaching in synagogues, telling story-driven truths to crowds of hungry people, and exposing the hypocrisy of the religious leaders, Jesus often validated His claim to be the Son of God. He fed thousands with paradigm-shifting truth and with miraculously multiplied loaves and fishes. Paralytics walked, blind men saw, the demon-possessed were delivered, dead bodies lived, and—most miraculous of all—sinners were forgiven and called to new life.

Transcending all the previous barriers to the presence of God, Jesus touched people and spoke to them face-to-face. Anyone could come to Jesus—without curtains or incense, animal sacrifices or priestly mediation. They could come to Him with their disease, their brokenness, their desperate desire to be healed of both illness and sinfulness. In welcoming the diseased, the sinners, the marginalized, the outcasts of society, Jesus made it clear that He gave the access to the Father that we need. He said, "I am the way, the truth, and the life. No one comes to the Father except through Me" (John 14:6).

To see Jesus was to see the Father. Jesus was the bridge between the outer court and the Most Holy Place. He could have healed from afar; he could have rebuked sin from a distance. But He was an up-close Savior. He spit in the mud and made a paste to smear over a blind man's eyes. He touched a man who had leprosy. It would have made anyone else ceremonially unclean—but when you are touched by the presence of God, your uncleanness is overwhelmed by His cleanness.

And really, this is the way the gospel works when we are reconciled to God. When we repent of our sin, and when God's saving grace turns our stony hearts into soft instruments of worship, the overwhelming holiness of Christ is credited to our account. It cancels out our indebtedness, heals our diseased hearts, and presents us holy before God. And not just holy in the way that we strive (and fail) to be holy, but holy as Jesus was and is and will always be: perfectly holy.

In every miracle, parable, and sermon, Jesus proved His claims of sonship and divinity, exposing the darkened hearts of men and exercising His authority over creation. He calmed storms in order to prove His deity while also demonstrating His power to override even the weakest faith. It is this restorative strength that I have learned to treasure the most. His presence can transcend and revive even the most threadbare faith.

## Calming Storms and Rebuking Doubt

Tucked in the fourteenth chapter of Matthew is one of my favorite stories about Jesus. Growing up in church, I heard countless sermons about this passage, but they always seemed to unfold with life lessons about Jesus calming the "storms" in life—storms like worry or financial strain. It always rang hollow—but how else could we connect a miraculous event like walking on water with our everyday lives?

On the heels of feeding thousands with a measly supply of bread and fish, Jesus made His disciples get in a boat and cross the Sea of Galilee while He slipped away to pray. Hours later, the disciples were struggling to keep their boat under control in a choppy sea. In the middle of the night, in the middle of the storm, in the middle of the sea, Jesus came walking across the water— miles from land. Understandably, the disciples were afraid. Losing control of the boat in a nighttime storm would have been reason enough for them to fear—but seeing someone walking on top of the water must have evoked a bit of outright terror! But when Jesus called out courage to them, His most impulsive follower begged to join Him on the water's surface. I always picture Peter jumping over the edge of the boat feetfirst. He walked out across the churning waves just like Jesus.

"But when [Peter] saw the strength of the wind, he was afraid. And beginning to sink he cried out, 'Lord, save me!'" (Matt. 14:30) Peter stopped looking at Jesus and instead fixed his gaze on what he feared.

And then Jesus exposed what was at the root of Peter's sinking: doubt. "You of little faith, why did you doubt?" (v. 31), He asked Peter—but there's a double purpose in His words. He admonished Peter's lack of faith while also reaching out to save him. He didn't let Peter sink to the bottom of the sea. He showed Peter what was in his heart while also delivering him from it. He can do the same for us.

Jesus calmed storms because He is God, and He delivers us from doubts because He is God *with us*. When Peter was sinking amid a raging sea because he couldn't see Jesus, God reminded him that He was with him. And when I was sinking to the bottom of disbelief because I couldn't see Jesus, God reached down to remind me that He was with me. At the weakest moment of my life, He reminded me that His grip was stronger than mine.

During my fifth year of unexplained chronic pain, I found myself entrenched in a mental battle. I was afraid of dying without knowing what was wrong with me, and I was afraid of living a long life of constant pain. I wasn't suicidal, but I couldn't think about turning forty, fifty, sixty in my worsening condition. Pain stole my rest, but the possibilities of both dying and living chipped at my sanity.

My family had walked with me through my years of pain, but they were as helpless to end it as I was. My husband often woke in the middle of the night when I did, but one particular night I didn't want to worry him with my fear. As my husband and son slept soundly, I shuffled across the living room floor, trying to quell the hysterics in my chest. With every breath, pain bore down on my spine, hips, ribcage. Anxiety squeezed around my throat while tears dripped off my cheeks. *Agony* is the only word I can use to describe what I felt. And for as much physical agony as I was feeling, my heart ached with its spiritual equivalent.

"Lord, save me!" was all I could cry out. It is the simplest of cries—the only plea that Peter could muster when doubt pulled his ankles down into the sea. "Lord, save me!" In a haze of pain, I thought of Peter and Jesus and their outstretched hands—and suddenly I knew. *Jesus was enough.* In my prayer for healing, I became aware of the presence of the Healer. He is the one I was after. He is the treasure in the field, the pearl of great price, the gift of the gospel. He is God with us—the very point of our reconciliation. He is both maker and master of the sea.

Jesus didn't calm the sea until He and Peter were back in the boat. He didn't still the churning waves until after He had gripped Peter's hand and proved Himself to be Peter's master. We might think we are ruled by the circumstances that tempt us to doubt, but Jesus is the master of us *and* our circumstances. He was the master of Peter *and* the sea. He was master of my pain *and* me. And as He did with Peter, He did not deliver me from pain but made certain that I knew who He was: present. Though I struggled to hold on to Him, He never lost His grip on me.

Eventually the panic in my chest stilled. The crushing pain continued, but with it came a determination to hold on to the truth that God was with me. For many nights afterward, I paced the floor with Peter and Jesus in my mind. Knowledge of Jesus's authority penetrated my darkest nights. His presence eclipsed my doubts, rebuking them while also overriding them.

I was reminded of all the things I had studied about Him in His Word for years leading up to this moment. He was with me because He had promised to be. Those days, weeks, months, and years I had spent absorbing what was true about the character of God culminated in one strong, transcendent truth on that dark night of body and soul: Immanuel. God was with me.

Over the course of my mysterious illness, I never once suffered alone. The Lord is with us, whether or not we are aware of His presence. He doesn't come and go or leave us waiting for Him to show up when we hurt. We do not have to call loudly and wait for His arrival. He is with us in our every pulse of pain or loneliness or fear. His solitary suffering on the cross removed the possibility of our suffering alone.

## At the Cross

Sometimes in metaphors, but most times in plain words, Jesus often told His disciples what would happen to Him. He wanted to prepare them for His arrest, death, and resurrection—and for the fallout. In a single chapter of Matthew we find specific statements about what would happen in the coming days:

> You know that the Passover takes place after two days, and the Son of Man will be handed over to be crucified. (Matt. 26:2)

> By pouring this fragrant oil on My body, she has prepared Me for burial. (Matt. 26:12)

> The Son of Man will go just as it is written about Him. (Matt. 26:24)

> Tonight all of you will run away because of Me. (Matt. 26:31)

> But after I have been resurrected, I will go ahead of you to Galilee. (Matt. 26:32).

Jesus assured the disciples that, though He would physically leave them through His death and subsequent resurrection and ascension, He would return for them. "I will not leave you as orphans," He promised. "I am coming to you" (John 14:18). He both promised them an admittance into the eternal presence of God and prepared them for a different manifestation of the presence of God. But first something had to take place that the disciples didn't want to hear about.

Jesus had been teaching and preaching about the kingdom of God, about His role in reconciling man to God, about His deity—all of which was blasphemy to the religious leaders. One of His most offensive teachings seemed to concern the temple where God's presence had previously dwelled: "Destroy this sanctuary, and I will raise it up in three days" (John 2:19). To the religious leaders, it was outlandish to speak of the destruction and rapid rebuilding of God's dwelling place. However, Jesus was referring to His own body rather than a physical building. He was saying that *He would be the place to meet with God.*

Jesus's subversive claims were full of a strange hope: "If anyone loves Me, he will keep My word. My Father will love him, and We will come to him and make Our home with him" (John 14:23). He was the avenue, the way, the mediation. He would replace the temple, because He was God. There was something better than the temple in Jerusalem: an even more tangible manifestation of the way God had chosen to dwell among His people. The first temple was His idea. This better one was, as well.

These "blasphemous" claims gave impetus to His enemies' plans to kill Jesus. The religious leaders, along with Judas (Jesus's friend-turned-enemy), plotted Jesus's death in secrecy, they thought—though Jesus knew that it had to be this way in order to fulfill all prophecy. And prophecy was clear about what would happen to the Suffering Servant.

Two prominent passages stand out in my mind, and probably in yours, when we think about the ancient words that laid out the downward-and-upward path that the Savior would take. Isaiah 53 and Psalm 22 are so specific that I wonder how the people of Israel missed them when they beheld Jesus on the cross.

The words of those passages are ominous, painful, sorrowful words. Through Isaiah, God had said, "He was despised and rejected by men, a man of suffering who knew what sickness was. He was like someone people turned away from; He was despised, and we didn't value Him" (Isa. 53:3). Certainly, some people understood that Jesus wasn't just any man. His disciples watched Him perform miracle after miracle, heard all His teachings and proclamations of deity, saw His *otherness*. Even so, they struggled to comprehend the truth about Him. And because He came in such a different way from what Israel was expecting, He wasn't valued the way that the Messiah might have otherwise been. Though the ones who witnessed His miracles might have believed, the tides of favor turned against Him when He stood before both the religious and governing authorities.

Betrayed by a friend and spirited away in the dark like a common criminal, Jesus was dragged before the authorities while compensated liars bore false witness about His supposed crimes. He admitted to what was true about Himself but otherwise made no defense. He just stood there, bound, and absorbed the untruths, the accusations, the blows and abuse. "He was oppressed and afflicted, yet He did not open His mouth. Like a lamb led to the slaughter and like a sheep silent before her shearers, He did not open His mouth" (Isa. 53:7).

He stood before the religious leaders and the governor, silent and guiltless, knowing that He would soon wear more than human skin. He would wear human *sin*. With hands that He had made, they pressed a crown of thorns into His skull. While the blood ran down His face, their eyes held a blindness that afflicts us all.

Until the blindness is removed, until the heart is made alive, until the corpse is resurrected, Jesus is just a man to the beholder. But this descent of His—this stooping low to scoop up all our darkness, all our blindness, all our hatred and rejection of the One who made us—this bending down to lift it onto Himself is precisely how the scales fall from our eyes. It's how dead hearts are injected with life, how ugliness is wiped clean, how the enemy becomes a beloved child. It was necessary—horrifyingly necessary.

Yet He Himself bore our sicknesses,
and He carried our pains;

119

> but we in turn regarded Him stricken,
> struck down by God, and afflicted.
> But He was pierced because of our transgressions,
> crushed because of our iniquities;
> punishment for our peace was on Him,
> and we are healed by His wounds.
>
> . . . . . . . . . . . . . . . . . . . . .
>
> And the LORD has punished Him
> for the iniquity of us all. (Isa. 53:4–6)

The crucifixion of Jesus spans only a few verses in each gospel. It's a short event in terms of word length. He was forced to carry His cross until His weakened, abused body couldn't bear the weight of it. He was nailed to the beams, and His crime was written on a sign for all to see: King of the Jews. He went willingly; He didn't resist. Prior to His arrest, He had sweated in a garden in agony while His disciples slept. He'd pleaded for another way, while knowing that He would obey His Father's will no matter the cost. And He knew the cost. *He* was the cost.

He hung on that cross—the cruelest form of execution at the time. It was a reprehensible way to die—one reserved for the lowest of criminals. He suffered physically, yes; crucifixion was an excruciating physical death. More than that, however, was what onlookers couldn't see. When Jesus hung on the cross, He said little, reserving His strength in order to cry out some of the most bone-chilling words in history. Haunting Hebrew words from the psalmist rushed from His mouth: "My God, my God, why have You forsaken me?" (Ps. 22:1)

The agony of the cross wasn't just physical. In dying a criminal's death, Jesus also took on the righteous wrath of God for all our sin. He who knew no sin *became sin*. He became sin and suffered alone in our place for our sins. My sins. Yours. We don't know the extent of forsakenness that Jesus experienced on the cross, but we do know that He carried both our sins and our sorrows so that we would be free to cry out to Him when the world goes dark.

## Never Alone

Janie and I met as teenagers. She walked with me through my infertility, and I supported her through her years of singleness. We both became ministry wives, then mothers. Janie seemed to be made for mothering. She was the one I turned to when my son was little and I was unsure how to deal with diaper rash or what to do about teething.

I celebrated with her when she called me to tell me the good news: baby number three was due in November. But, four months later, the phone rang with the news that her baby was dead. He had died in the womb—had stopped moving and growing without notice.

Living out of state, I couldn't be with Janie in the hospital when she delivered her lifeless son and made friends with a grief that I hope never to meet personally. The next day, though, I sat in her living room and wept with her. I gripped her hands but didn't know how to help to hold her grief. She spoke first. "I'm so grateful I don't have to go through this alone," she said to me. "Jesus suffered on the cross alone so that I would never have to suffer alone."

I was paralyzed by her confession. I had come to offer compassion and hope, but now I sat dumbfounded by the truth she had spoken. How had I missed this huge piece of what was accomplished at the crucifixion? The segregation of man and God was resolved at the cross when Jesus bore the full brunt of God's wrath for our sin. And because it was finished then and there, the redeemed will never, ever experience that separation. Janie didn't suffer alone, because Jesus suffered in her place on

the cross. This is grace upon grace—the gift of presence upon the
gift of salvation. Jesus accomplished both at the cross. The apostle
Paul affirmed this truth with poetic punch:

> He did not even spare His own Son
> but offered Him up for us all;
> how will He not also with Him grant us everything?
> Who can bring an accusation against God's elect?
> God is the One who justifies.
> Who is the one who condemns?
> Christ Jesus is the One who died,
> but even more, has been raised;
> He also is at the right hand of God
> and intercedes for us.
> Who can separate us from the love of Christ?
> Can affliction or anguish or persecution
> or famine or nakedness or danger or sword?
> As it is written:
> Because of You
> we are being put to death all day long;
> we are counted as sheep to be slaughtered.
> No, in all these things we are more than victorious
> through Him who loved us.
> For I am persuaded that not even death or life,
> angels or rulers,
> things present or things to come, hostile powers,
> height or depth, or any other created thing
> will have the power to separate us
> from the love of God that is in Christ Jesus our Lord! (Rom.
>     8:32–39)

Grieving with hope, my friend spoke gospel truth to me that
day while her life broke apart around her. She wasn't alone in her

suffering. God was with her—really with her—in every moment of her grief, because Jesus had climbed on the cross alone, borne her sin alone, and died alone. His resurrection meant that she had hope for her own resurrection. And she could hope for the resurrection of her baby boy, for whom there is no pain or suffering anymore—only light and life with Christ.

Jesus's solitary suffering cannot be overstated, for in it is the great exchange that takes place for the redeemed. Each of us must answer for this deep, sin-wide chasm between ourselves and the God who made a way to bridge the chasm. There are only two options. Either we bear the weight of our own sin in an eternity that will be forever divorced from His loving presence, or we believe that the forsakenness of Christ alone on the cross was enough for our redemption so that we may enjoy the presence of God both now and forever.

Do you believe not only that you need Jesus's payment for your sins but that His payment is enough for you and for the deepest need of your heart? You do not have to face an eternity alone without His loving presence, and you do not have to walk through suffering alone. Jesus suffered the brunt of God's wrath so that you might know the presence of that same God who is both fire and fury as well as faithfulness and love. We couldn't bridge the chasm—but it was always His plan to be the bridge Himself. It was always His plan to lay down His life and take it up again. Our hope is upheld by the power of the resurrection.

## A Borrowed Grave for the Crusher of Snakes

But before there could be a resurrection, there had to be death—the death to end death. On the day Jesus died, the world darkened at noon. As the earth trembled and broke open, the need for man's protection from God the Father became, in one last gasping breath, completely null and void.

Jesus's last breath signified the ending not just of His life but of all the obstacles that separated man from God. In the heart of the city of Jerusalem, the temple curtain ripped from top to bottom when Jesus died. Designed to protect man from the holiness of God, the fabric was rent all the way down. A. W. Tozer said, "It was this last veil which was rent when our Lord gave up the ghost on Calvary, and the sacred writer explains that this rending of the veil opened the way for every worshiper in the world to come by the new and living way straight into the divine Presence."[1] Jesus died, and the curtain split open wide. In one moment, its presence became completely, eternally unnecessary. Jesus's sacrifice on a cross allowed any man to approach the Father for forgiveness of sins.

Unlike the countless gutted lambs and goats that had paid for sins in the past, Jesus's lifeless body wasn't rendered useless postmortem. Death wouldn't win—couldn't win. The garden snake of Genesis 3 may have struck His heel, but the One who was crushed by the weight of the cross was also the snake-crusher. He wouldn't be held captive by death. Jesus wasn't Immanuel, God with us, for just a little while. He was God with us even after His death. His grave was borrowed, for His stay would be short. "They made His grave with the wicked and with a rich man at His death, although He had done no violence and had not spoken deceitfully" (Isa. 53:9).

The death sentence couldn't defeat Him; the grave couldn't hold Him. The Father was satisfied with the atonement that had been made by His Son. The fullest expression of God's presence had dwelled among us in order to redeem us from our slavery to sin and to bring us to God. On His shoulders was the weight of every angry, selfish, lustful, greedy, murderous thought and

---

1. A. W. Tozer, *The Pursuit of God: The Human Thirst for the Divine* (1948; repr., Camp Hill, PA: Christian Publications, 1993), 34.

action. He wore our rejection, our self-worship, our hatred of God, our loyalty to the enemy, our love for the fruit of Eden's tree, our commitment to find satisfaction outside of God. And when He gave Himself for our sin, it was enough. He was enough.

> Yet the LORD was pleased to crush Him severely.
> When You make Him a restitution offering,
> He will see His seed, He will prolong His days,
> and by His hand, the LORD's pleasure will be accomplished.
> He will see it out of His anguish,
> and He will be satisfied with His knowledge.
> My righteous Servant will justify many,
> and He will carry their iniquities. (Isa. 53:10–11)

Jesus's sacrifice at the cross reconciles us to God and enables us to know and freely enjoy His presence. By suffering alone in our place, Jesus has ensured that we will never walk through sorrow or grief or pain in solitude. Whatever dark valley you are walking through, if you have placed your faith in Christ, you will never endure suffering alone. Jesus made the way for us to know God's presence always.

### Discussion Questions

1. To see Jesus was to see the Father (see John 1:18). How is this radically different from the way that God's people approached Him before the birth of Christ?
2. Peter's simple cry, "Lord, save me!" in Matthew 14:30 was all he could muster when he was sinking in the Sea of Galilee. What does Jesus's response reveal about Peter's faith, and why is it the rebuke that we need when we're afraid?
3. In this chapter, we read the crucifixion story through the words of the prophet Isaiah. Read Isaiah 53 and write a few

sentences about the ways that Jesus carried your sins and sorrows to the cross.

4. Glenna tells the story of her friend's tragic stillbirth and the surprising encouragement that her friend offered in her grief. Do you find comfort in the truth that we never suffer alone? Why or why not?

5. The sacrifice of Jesus at the cross provided not only atonement for our sins but also the gift of God's presence forever. Have you trusted that Jesus's sacrifice is enough to cover your sin and to assure that you never suffer alone? Share your testimony briefly.

# 8

# Always Present

*And remember, I am with you always, to the end of the age.*

—MATTHEW 28:20

I live in an extremely flat part of the country with no snow-capped mountains or icy cold, trickling streams to redeem winter for us. The trees are bare, the fields are bare, and the farm land that surrounds us is flat and desolate. Gray earth, gray sky—it's hard to find the horizon sometimes.

When spring comes, it comes quietly at first. It's a whisper of green, a blush of pink, a shift from sharp wind to breeze. And then one day you wake up and the world is on fire with a painter's palette, and you remember that no matter what drags down your heart with grief, seasons change and hope can rise with the morning sun.

Yet hope wasn't that clear-cut after the crucifixion. Jesus died. I think that sometimes we glaze over that truth because it's familiar. But think about it for a moment. He *died*. No more breathing. He inhaled and exhaled one last time on the cross, and while the world reacted with tremulous groanings, earthquakes, miracles, and torn curtains, any spark of hope in Jesus's followers must have nearly been snuffed out. There was no more breath in the Son of God.

And then, suddenly, there was.

Buried and then unburied, dead and then alive, breathless and then breathing, Jesus was resurrected by the power of the same God who promised to be with you and me. His resurrection was proof of life—a guarantee of all the promises Jesus had made. One of those promises didn't come to fruition until He left the earth to sit down next to His Father in heaven when His work was done—final, acceptable, and resolved. He promised to send the Holy Spirit so that His followers would never be alone.

Prior to His death, Jesus told His disciples,

> And I will ask the Father, and He will give you another Counselor to be with you forever. He is the Spirit of truth. The world is unable to receive Him because it doesn't see Him or know Him. But you do know Him, because He remains with you and will be in you. ( John 14:16–17)

Jesus knew His disciples would be afraid in His absence, and they were. Toward the end of the gospel narratives, you find them hiding out in rooms with locked doors.

That's why, even after appearing to them freshly resurrected, Jesus reminded them of His continual presence with them even during His physical absence. He would keep His promise, as the Spirit would be with them always—even to the end of the age.

In every verse of the grand redemption story, the people of God are given the presence of God. So, even though Jesus's friends were afraid, He assured them that He would continue to be with them. God would give them—and us—presence in the nearness of the Holy Spirit.

As did the incarnation, the coming of the Holy Spirit spelled another huge shift in the patterns of presence throughout the history of God with us. God spoke to the people collectively, through prophets, through smoke and fire, through the curtain of the temple. Then Jesus appeared in the flesh—lived, died, rose, returned to heaven. The third and final way that God kept His promise to be present on earth was through the gift of the Holy Spirit to every believer. Individually—not just corporately, and not just face-to-face with only a handful of people in the Middle East for thirty-three years. (Though those years had such a history-splitting impact that we can't say they weren't enough.)

No, now He would reside *within* every believer for all time—a promise that extends thousands of years forward to people like me, who can't seem to remember that in the Lord I have everything I need.

## Treasure in the Waiting Room

Have you ever wondered what it was like during those three quiet days between the crucifixion and the resurrection? Those three days may have held more longing, yearning, and suffocating hope than all the silent four hundred years before Jesus's birth. Jesus's followers sat in a room with the doors locked. After all, Jesus did say, "If they persecuted Me, they will also persecute you" (John 15:20). Even after the discovery of the empty tomb, surely the locked room was heavy with fear. What would happen next?

They'd seen Him die; they knew He'd been buried. If the One who calmed storms and erased leprosy could be killed before their eyes, where was hope? One disciple said, "We were hoping that He was the One who was about to redeem Israel. Besides all this, it's the third day since these things happened" (Luke 24:21). You can feel the hope draining out of him as he says those words. The disciples doubted His promises to them. I would have. I can't imagine their joy and disbelief, then, when Jesus joined them, appearing in the locked room in a body that they remembered, which was now marked with scars that should have been theirs. And ours.

In the tight places of deferred hope, doubting God's promises can become a full-time job. It doesn't take much for us to take on the occupation of disbelief. It takes much less than a crucified Savior for us to doubt that He will hold up His promises to be good and faithful. All it takes is the inconvenient act of waiting.

Waiting is quiet. It's lonely. Waiting feels like standing still, and standing still feels like the opposite of sanctification. It's work, but it doesn't look like the progressive, growing-in-faith kind of work. It's more like treading water—struggling to stay upright. In the weary work of waiting, we hear a serpent's hiss and wonder whether we misunderstood God. Did He really say that He is good? Is He able to do what He said? How can He be loving to us when he defers our hopes?

We have two options when it comes to waiting. We can question why God is withholding something from us, or we can look for what He is teaching us about Himself as we wait. In our waiting, we can discover what we're actually waiting for. It's like going to the doctor for indigestion and getting a life-saving heart transplant in the waiting room. God can use our unfulfilled desires to reveal what we need the most. It's always Him.

I thought I was waiting for physical healing, for another child, for our life in ministry to become successful (or at least to stop failing). I prayed for those things until I ran out of words. Months and years yielded nothing more than quiet mornings with my Bible open on my lap. I watched the sun rise through the tulip trees and wondered if my life would ever be any different. Would God still be good if it wasn't?

Waiting was not what I had prayed for, but waiting was what I needed. Slowly, the open Bible in my morning routine reshaped my heart. In pain, I learned to ask, "Who are You?" when I opened my tattered copy of the Scriptures. The answer was a comfort: He was Good. Faithful. Near, not far off. Holy. Transcendent. Compassionate. Slow to anger. Immanuel. Just. Eternal. Present.

Every time I asked the question, the answers were sufficient. When I wanted something extrabiblical, like a promise that I would have another child, the Scriptures were sufficient in their refusal to bend to my will. God has given us everything we need to know in order to endure. We do not need an extra word from the Lord, and when we ask for it, we deny that He is enough for us. When we demand that His words reveal a "special" truth that is specific to our personal circumstances, we proclaim the insufficiency of both the Scriptures and the God who spoke them.

When we change our approach to Scripture from "What's in it for me?" to "Who are You?" we position our hearts to believe that God is enough for us. In that posture of humility, we find the fulfillment that comes from knowing that He is. The answer to my question gradually rewired my desires. The tenets of God's character unearthed in me a longing that had been masked by my earthly yearnings. Looking to Him in Scripture revealed that He was the object of my longing. And thankfully for me, and for you, and for all who believe, He has already given us Himself. All that we need. More than we need. Enough to keep us full while also drawing us back for more.

When you wonder if you'll ever have joy again, He is enough for you. When there is no margin for hope, run to the Word, friend. Hope is bursting off the pages, for every page is about Him. Let Him tell you who He is. Circumstances ebb and flow, but He never does. He has never withheld what we need of Him. He is the one we are waiting for, and He is the one we've been given.

The disciples may have despaired in the room behind the locked door, but just when three days seemed too long to wait, hope came and stood among them and reminded them what true victory looked like. "As the Father has sent Me, I also send you," Jesus said. "After saying this, He breathed on them and said, 'Receive the Holy Spirit'" ( John 20:21–22)

## Breath of Heaven

For forty days, the resurrected Jesus spoke to His followers. It seems that well over five hundred people witnessed the evidence of His victory over the grave (see 1 Cor. 15:6). During those forty days, Jesus restored His friend Peter who had denied Him, encouraged His disciples, and commissioned them to take the message of His kingdom to all the earth. Some of His final earthly words to them were this: "And remember, I am with you always, to the end of the age" (Matt. 28:20) Charging them to be His witnesses throughout the world, He then ascended to heaven before their very eyes (see Acts 1:8–9). How could He make a promise of presence and then leave? He had every intention of keeping that promise. After His return to heaven, the events of Acts 2 unfolded with a remarkable, supernatural fulfillment of His promise. During the Jewish festival of Pentecost, Jesus's followers were gathered together when a sound like a violent wind came from above and filled the house where they were staying.

Flickering flames appeared and rested on the waiting believers. They were filled with the Holy Spirit and began to speak in other languages—an ability that Luke credits to the Spirit in Acts 2:4. Many different groups of people heard their native tongues being spoken, and it stirred up a lot of confusion among them. Our beloved, impulsive, water-walking former Jesus-denier, Peter, stepped in to explain that the gift of the Holy Spirit for all believers was the fulfillment of the prophecies of Joel, who said, "After this [God] will pour out [His] Spirit on all humanity . . . [He] will even pour out [His] Spirit on the male and female slaves in those days" (Joel 2:28, 29). There would be no distinction. Every believer in Christ would receive the gift of the Spirit.

As Peter explained at Pentecost, Jesus's promise was fulfilled: "Therefore, since [Jesus] has been exalted to the right hand of God and has received from the Father the promised Holy Spirit,

He has poured out what you both see and hear" (Acts 2:33). The Spirit is, from this point forward, present among the people of God. According to New Testament writers such as Paul, Peter, and John, believers should both expect and depend on the Spirit's involvement in their lives. His presence in the heart of the Christian is our guarantee that justification is sure, that sanctification is ongoing, and that future glorification is secured.

While Christ intercedes for us and the Father works sovereignly, this third member of the Godhead dwells in us to help us to persevere until the day we are face-to-face with our triune God in heaven. The three persons of the Trinity are not trading off roles, as some suggest.[1] Rather, they each work in harmonious unity for God's glory and pleasure and for our good. The presence of the Spirit in us is the down payment of the promise of full, unhindered access to the presence of God in heaven. We have the presence of God in *us* now as a guarantee that one day we will be with *Him* forever.

This knowledge upholds me when ministry feels lonely, when my body is wrecked by pain, when the longings of my heart seem to go unanswered. What is truer than the way we feel is the ministry of the Spirit, who groans for us when we don't know how to pray. What transcends sorrow is knowing that Jesus is determined to present all believers pure and spotless before the Father. What aids our perseverance is confidence that the Father loves us because we get to wear the righteousness of Jesus. We may have sung the song of dissatisfaction to Him, but because of His commitment to keep His promises, He sings songs of joy over us.

When, in unfailing kindness, the Father led us to repentance,

---

1. "Modalism claims that there is one person who appears to us in three different forms. . . . The fatal shortcoming of modalism is the fact that it must deny the personal relationships within the Trinity that appear in so many places in Scripture." Wayne Grudem, *Systematic Theology: An Introduction to the Biblical Doctrine* (Grand Rapids: Zondervan, 1994), 242.

He accepted Jesus's death in place of ours. Now when He sees us, He no longer recounts the ways we have rejected Him. Though we have proclaimed, in anger or despair, "You are not enough for me," He has scattered the notes of our dirge so widely that they cannot be recomposed. Now when He looks on us, He sees the beauty of Christ and hears *His* song of obedience. We will spend all our days learning to sing it well, and His presence with us guarantees that we will learn the tune. This is the power of the gospel. This is the gift of the Spirit of God that came rushing down, breathed out from the lips of Jesus and poured out on everyone who loves Him until the end.

In the beginning, God breathed life into a man who was created from dust. In the beginning of the church, He breathed out His presence into His people. His intent was to be with us, and His plans are never thwarted.

### Joints and Marrow, Soul and Spirit

What does it mean to enjoy the presence of Someone whom we can't see? The answer isn't new, but it's one that we need. Our primary means of enjoying the presence of God is His Word. The Bible is *God's chosen means* of revelation, and we must submit to His authority by knowing Him in the way He has given us to know Him. Coupled with prayer, opening our Bibles should be nonnegotiable in our efforts to take advantage of God's presence in our lives.

The Bible is not like other books—and before you insert a well-deserved *duh* right here, let me rephrase that with the words of the writer of Hebrews: "For the word of God is living and effective and sharper than any double-edged sword, penetrating as far as the separation of soul and spirit, joints and marrow. It is able to judge the ideas and thoughts of the heart" (Heb. 4:12). The Word is living and active. It transforms and renews our minds, resulting in obedience. It reveals where we have sinned and shows us how to repent. This book holds the words of the Creator—powerful words that have an eternity-changing impact on those who open their eyes and ears to it. We have staked our eternity on the words of this book, and we pattern our lives after the commands within it.

A visiting missionary once told a story to our church about a tribal chief in Papua New Guinea who heard the gospel story for the first time. After hearing the good news of Jesus, the chief said, "I *knew* that there was Someone, but I did not know His name!" While we can be moved by the beauty of a sunset and know that Someone must have created the universe, we need the Word of God to tell us who Jesus is and how we can be saved.[2]

The Spirit is the one who helps us to understand, remember, and obey the Word of God. Here's what Jesus said about that:

> When the Spirit of truth comes, He will guide you into all the truth. For He will not speak on His own, but He will speak whatever He hears. He will also declare to you what is to come. He will glorify Me, because He will take from what is Mine and declare it to you. Everything the Father has is Mine. This is why I told you that He takes from what is Mine and will declare it to you. (John 16:13–15)

What an incredible gift He promised, and what an incredible gift we have received! The Spirit of God lives in us, prompts us with truth from the Father, helps us to understand the words of the Lord, and enables us to grow in spiritual maturity.

Because of Jesus's work at the cross and gift of the Spirit, the

---

2. In theological terms, the sunset is *general* revelation—God has revealed Himself in creation, and because of this, we are without excuse for our sins (see Rom. 1:20). God's Word is *particular* revelation: the means by which we know God, the gospel, and Jesus. See Grudem, *Systematic Theology*, 149.

apostle Paul said that "we all, with unveiled faces, are looking as in a mirror at the glory of the Lord and are being transformed into the same image from glory to glory; this is from the Lord who is the Spirit" (2 Cor. 3:18). You and I are included in that beautiful promise! We get to see the Lord in His glory, through the gift of the Word, because the Spirit dwells in us and helps us to see Him as He has revealed Himself to us.

When you sit down to read the Bible, you lean deeply into the presence of God. You hear about His character from His mouth first so that you recognize it in your circumstances later. When you dig through passages and parse them for what you can learn about God, you acknowledge that knowing God will change you. Prayer and Bible-reading give us the opportunity to say, "Lord, this is the way I can know You. Whatever You want me to know about You is held within Your book. Help me to understand it, to remember it, to obey it." And because the Spirit lives in you, you *can* understand it and you *can* obey it! When you look back on your life and see growth and obedience, you can know with confidence that the Spirit has been at work.

When Jesus prayed to the Father in John 17:17, "Sanctify them by the truth; Your word is truth," He thereby encouraged us to look to Scripture for all truth. We do not need to look for extra-biblical insights that might speak to our specific circumstances, nor should we depend on "revelation" that does not agree with Scripture. The Word of God is sufficient and gives us everything we need to know about God. If you want to be comforted by His presence, then understand the character of the One who is with you by engaging with Him in His Word.

It matters that He is with us in our every attempt to read our Bibles. The words of the Lord breathe out instruction, encouragement, necessary rebuke, hope, and comfort. Regular exposure to the Word renews our minds as its truths permeate every cobwebbed corner of our hearts and minds by the Spirit's power.

With His help, not only do we read and absorb the Word, but our souls are indelibly imprinted with its truth. Only the Word of God and the indwelling of the Spirit can reach down that deeply and separate joints and marrow, soul and spirit.

## He Is No Stand-In

My grandmother suffered tremendously from Alzheimer's Disease for six years. Her struggle was strange and difficult to watch. She lost her motor skills first; and, as the disease progressed, so did the loss of her capabilities. Speech went, and then cognition. The only times she truly responded were when my mother turned on a televised church service for her to watch on Sunday mornings. Sandy Willson and Charles Swindoll were favorites of hers, and my grandmother often wept while they preached. She had long left behind her dependable moments of lucidity, but the preaching of the Word had a longer-lasting hold on her than most anything else.

Not long before my grandmother died, a home health nurse stopped by to visit for the sole purpose of singing to her. She asked my mother what hymns my grandmother had enjoyed earlier in life, and then she sat down facing my grandmother, knee to knee. She grasped both of her hands, looked deeply into her eyes, and in a deep, rich voice belted out the words of "How Great Thou Art." My grandmother found a way out of her confusion and made eye contact with the singer. Unable to speak but trying desperately to sing along, she nodded emphatically in a way she hadn't done in many, many months. Something within her resonated with the words she was hearing. The Scriptures, the hymns, the sermons touched a part of her that pushed against the disease and responded.

Just a few weeks before she died, I watched my grandmother stare into space. She seemed to respond to things she saw that we didn't. She was agitated a lot, restless, which is not uncommon for Alzheimer's patients. She was locked in a world that we couldn't penetrate and that she couldn't escape. It grieved us to witness her isolated decline.

And *yet*. She wasn't alone in that world of confusion. My grandmother had loved Jesus, long and hard. Her money, her time, her affection, her home—all were spent as an outpouring of her love for Christ and of His for her. She gave every morning first to the Lord who had captured her heart. The Holy Spirit had livened her dead heart by grace through saving faith in Christ. Alzheimer's could not separate her from the love of Christ. Even in her isolated globe of confusion, she was never alone. God did not abandon her in the darkness of dementia, because He always keeps His promise of presence.

The Holy Spirit does not depart from the ones He has sealed for an eternal inheritance. My grandmother's inheritance is God Himself; He certainly would not leave her when her mind was incapable of remembering Him. Perhaps it was when she needed Him the most. The same is true for us. The presence of God through the indwelling of the Holy Spirit means that we are truly never alone. It matters that the Spirit is with us. He isn't just a stand-in or a substitute. He is the surety we can hold on to. He is the guarantee of our new life and the down payment of our eternal one. And He's with us in each corner of our sanctification and glorification.

## Filled with the Fullness of God

Sometimes it's hard to be certain that God is with us, especially when we're enduring an open-ended period of waiting. Difficult life circumstances press against our theology, and unfortunately we often let our emotions tell us what's true. I've had days when my Bible seems dry and irrelevant. If I allow my feelings about the Lord to drive my theology, I will end up believing a false gospel whose anthem bears an uncanny resemblance to that timeless song of dissatisfaction. If I get up one morning and can't attach any emotion to what I'm reading in the Bible, then it must mean that God is far away, right? He just *feels* far sometimes. But this is where we must let Scripture guide us, for Scripture is truth—not our feelings about it.

After Pentecost, Peter preached his inaugural sermon, pleading with his listeners to "repent and turn back, so that your sins may be wiped out, that seasons of refreshing may come from the presence of the Lord" (Acts 3:19). According to Peter, the one who has repented and whose sin has been wiped away will be refreshed by the presence of the Lord. Being a believer in Christ implies that you have His presence. Even if you don't *feel* that you do, hold on to the truth that you do.

Paul prayed a similar truth over the Ephesian Christians, acknowledging that understanding the depth of Christ's love fills the believer with the fullness of God (see Eph. 3:18–19). *Filled with the fullness of God.* It's not as if God gave us a mere whisper or hint of His presence. The Holy Spirit is not a placeholder until Jesus returns; He is a person of the Godhead. God did not hold back when He sent us the Spirit. While we wait out trials, suffering, or deferred hopes, the Spirit is with us to help us press on in faith even when the answers aren't what we hope. He helps us to hold fast to the truth that God is with us, loves us, and is for us.

The promise of God's nearness with you as you wait is not a sentiment. Christian, you are filled with the fullness of God. You can have every confidence that He is with you constantly. You cannot be empty when you are filled with the fullness of God. And it is His nearness that will preserve you through suffering and will keep your heart firmly planted in His Word. Though you may wait with longing or may ache with suffering, He has not abandoned you. He is very, very near.

## Discussion Questions

1. How was the gift of the Holy Spirit to every believer a shift from the way God's people had historically understood His presence?

2. In seasons of waiting, we often fret over why God is taking so long. How might we reframe our approach to waiting on the Lord in light of verses such as Psalm 25:5–9; 62:5; and 130:5–6?

3. Why is the Bible sufficient to answer our questions about God and ourselves?

4. How does study of and meditation on Scripture help us to enjoy the presence of God? What is the Holy Spirit's role in this?

5. Paul tells us that we as believers have been filled with the fullness of God (see Eph. 3:19). What does this mean for us when we face unfulfilled longings and deferred hopes?

# Part 3

---

# God's Presence
# Now and Forever

# 9

# You Are Enough for Me

*Though wounded by sorrow and grief, [the believer]*
*finds rest in the spiritual comfort of his God.*

—JOHN CALVIN

Is there a place for grief in the life of the believer? Can we hold lament in one hand and belief in God's sufficiency in the other? Can you proclaim with your mind that God is enough while your broken heart stumbles a few steps behind? As we've traveled the path of God's promise of presence throughout Scripture, we've watched Him consistently demonstrate His sufficiency to people who struggled to believe Him. In their trials, they wondered whether God would be enough for them. In our trials, we wonder whether God will be enough for us. Lament is the very thing that can lead us to faith in God's sufficiency. It is perhaps in the depths of sorrow and suffering that we best understand God's nearness. And that is when we learn that His nearness is enough.

As my mysterious pain condition worsened, my husband and I found ourselves in yet another season of waiting and discontent. For years we had tarried on an adoption waiting list that never changed, and after a decade of painful church work, we found more brokenness around the corner of every new and puzzling conflict. It seemed that everything we touched turned to ashes. Unconvinced that leaving was the right answer, we stayed. We were weary, hopeless, and desperate for something in our lives to have a good return.

Learning contentment is a slow process. Our flesh longs to be satisfied by tangible gifts—by things we can point to and say, "God is good." It requires far more faith and humility for us to point to our lack and bless the Lord for His goodness. Each day of waiting brings new opportunities to treasure God Himself more than the tangible things He might give us. It's not that the gift and the Giver are mutually exclusive objects of affection; it's that our obsession with the former precludes our enjoyment of the latter. More than I needed peace or health or children, I needed to learn contentment in God and His good, faithful character. No amount of fringe benefits, no matter how sweet, will assuage our need for God alone. We may mask our desires with other good things, but in the end they are poor substitutions for the One we were created to worship.

Even so, sometimes God does bring about the things that we long and pray for, and we can praise Him for His kindness and for the end of hopes deferred. And sometimes, after we praise Him, we realize that the gifts can never replace the Giver and that it's a good thing we're learning to hold fast to the One who holds fast to us.

## The Psalms Are Where You Go

After five years on a waiting list, we finally got the call we'd been waiting for. We packed all night and left at first light, excited and nervous about what we would find at the end of our seven-hour trip. Cautious, hopeful, afraid, excited—being matched in adoption is a nervy feeling that's hard to explain without overusing tired words. When we stepped off the hospital elevator and I put my hand on the doorknob to my future, I was afraid of the potential answer to prayer that would be on the other side of the door.

I loved the baby in the hospital bassinet as soon as I saw him. Simple, fierce maternal love doesn't have to be biological to be real. And that's what made it so hard for us when, after a week of loving and caring for him, the phone rang and everything began to unravel. No one knew why the process had become so complicated so quickly, but the social workers, the attorneys, the family—everyone suggested that we keep the baby while we could. We'd read books and attended classes on trauma and attachment. Determined to love him while we could, we kept him without any guarantee that keeping him permanently was an option for us. Every night, I rocked him to sleep in the corner of the quiet spare bedroom. We didn't have the heart to turn it into a full nursery.

I remember his baby weight against my chest—a feeling of warmth that I cherish and miss today. "Will I have to give you up tomorrow?" I'd whisper before swaddling him tightly and laying him gently in his crib. I'd watch his face relax and his eyes move beneath his lids as he slipped into that infant sleep with its grunts and quick, shallow breaths. I always lingered next to his crib, my hand on his chest. It was my nightly liturgy—a series of desperate prayers for the baby in the crib.

Being the mother of a newborn brings a special kind of exhaustion. Like most new moms, I got up every two hours for feedings throughout the night; coupled with my chronic pain and emotional distress, I could feel the wear and tear on my body. The lack of sleep, the ever-present fear of losing our new son, the persistent physical pain—it was too much. My thoughts felt frayed and hard to capture, my prayers threaded together with only a loose coherence. My mind was clouded with what I now know to call "brain fog"—a symptom of underlying conditions that are brought on by chronic inflammation in the body.[1]

After nearly a decade that I had spent trying, failing, and trying again to seek the Lord in His Word, the habit of daily discipline took hold of my days. I had no other well to draw from that would answer the grief and uncertainty in my heart. Providentially, I landed in the Psalms, and I stayed there for eighteen months, long after our ordeal was resolved.

When your fears or grief or pain control your every waking thought, when every morning is a question mark and every night a potential last one, the Psalms are where you go. God gave us an indispensable gift in the hundred and fifty poems at the center of our Bible. The inspired voices of King David, Ethan, Asaph, Moses, and others cover every gamut of emotion while gently tilting our chins toward the face of our faithful, present God.

I dove into the Psalms full force, reading them one after the other and pressing the desperate words of the psalmists into my journal with anger, fear, and despair. The resonant words of dramatic lament were ones that I understood. No one was after my life, but life as I knew it seemed to be one breath away from utter despair. I understood David's feelings of hopelessness. I agreed with his "how long, O LORDs" and felt the grit of his eyes that were weary from crying.

Yet for every day of potential loss, there was new mercy to be found. For every time I agreed with the psalmist in his grief, I also found a flickering light of hope that pointed to God's historically faithful love. I went to the Psalms for commiseration in my grief. But I came away with the hope that transcends every broken heart: the hope that God was with me in my suffering.

---

1. Valencia Higuera, "6 Possible Causes of Brain Fog," HealthLine, last updated June 14, 2017, https://www.healthline.com/health/brain-fog.

## Immanuel for Always

Days turned into weeks and months. The baby grew and hit milestones that we celebrated with smiles and tears. I was afraid that every first was also a last. The holidays were unbearably hard. No one knew how to handle the newest member of our family. Buy him gifts? Include him in family photos? What if he was whisked away from us after the holidays? Love might mean holding him loosely. No one wanted us to deal with the reminders of a child who'd been lost to us.

Decorating for Christmas that year broke my heart. We turned on our favorite Christmas music, dragged out the decorations, poured cups of cider. I wept the entire time. I could think of no place I'd rather be and also rather not be. Months into the ordeal, we still had no clear answers. The outcome didn't look favorable.

In the midst of twinkling lights and scattered boxes of décor, my seven-year-old son picked up an ornament that he'd made the year before. It was a simple piece of pale blue construction paper that I'd laminated and strung with ribbon. I'd forgotten about it. Scrawled across the front was one simple word: *Immanuel*. At Christmas we notice His name everywhere, as well we should. But on this particular Christmas, I didn't need a guarantee that things would turn out well. I needed to remember that no matter what the next day held, God was with us.

I didn't understand the *why* behind any of it. I still don't. But studying the scrappy blue ornament reminded me of what I'd nearly forgotten. Immanuel made certain that we would always know the presence of the Lord. When I remembered His nearness, the *who* mattered much more than the *why*. His presence secured our perseverance. He was with us, and that was all we needed to know.

Jesus wasn't just Immanuel in the manger or on the Galilean hillsides. He is Immanuel for always. *God with us* wasn't confined to Israel during Jesus's time on earth. *God with us* is for now. He is with us now! Believing that His promise to be with us transcends our suffering is vital to enduring the various trials we face in life. God's presence is the key to perseverance. Confidence in His faithfulness is the coat that you wear when the cold winds of grief pull at your faith. Belief in His commitment to never forsake you is protection in the battle to find joy in your suffering.

I cried out with David,

> Protect me, God, for I take refuge in You.
> I said to Yahweh, "You are my Lord;
> I have nothing good besides You." (Ps. 16:1–2)

And I believed it with David—I truly had nothing good apart from the nearness of God. Life would be a shambles without His persistent presence. Pressing into the Scriptures on each morning of possible loss was the way for me to experience His presence. Had I ignored the Bible on my coffee table during those months of fear and uncertainty, I would surely have missed the life-changing reality of God's presence with me.

To experience God's presence is not to experience some ghostly premonition of wellbeing. No, it's much deeper than that, thankfully. And much, much stronger. Experiencing God's presence during crisis is pouring the truth of His good character into your doubting heart. It's letting Him tell you who He is through His Word. It's hearing in His voice on the page what your eyes can't always see in your circumstances. It's beholding the imprint of His character in the words He has given and being changed by them. You may not understand what He is doing in the tattered time line of your life, but He is still being good to you by being *with* you in it.

Every promise of God's perpetual presence in the Psalms is medicine for the broken heart. Every truth about His covenant love seals up the cracks of splintering faith. Though I couldn't see what was coming, I didn't need to see it. I just needed to know that He was with me in it. And therein is the paradoxical gift of suffering: confidence in the presence of God. Sometimes He covers our eyes so that we'll learn what His voice sounds like. Faith is only faith when it can't see what's up ahead but trusts anyway.

I would not have absorbed the truth about His faithfulness so deeply if I had not had to lean so heavily on it. Sometimes the valley of the shadow is where we need to walk in order to comprehend His constancy. Where else can you know for sure that He is with you? If you live only by quiet waters, you don't need to lean so hard on His rod and staff. It's on the fearfully long roads, it's when you're faced with what you're most afraid of, it's down in the valley of the shadow of death that you know in your bones that He is with you.

On those mornings when I wasn't sure what news the day would bring, I learned to sing with the psalmists that the Lord was my portion and that He was enough. If He could preserve me through the scariest days of my life, then He was truly all that I needed. When the good ending didn't seem likely, His nearness was my anchor. As I prayed the psalmists' words, I reminded the Lord of all the ways He had promised to be with His people—not because He needed to be reminded, but because I did.

When God promises to be with His people, nothing can thwart His good purposes.

Make Your ways known to me, Lord;
teach me Your paths.
Guide me in Your truth and teach me,
for You are the God of my salvation;
I wait for You all day long.
Remember, Lord, Your compassion
and Your faithful love,
for they have existed from antiquity.

Do not remember the sins of my youth
or my acts of rebellion;
in keeping with Your faithful love, remember me
because of Your goodness, LORD. (Ps. 25:4–7)

In the grip of sorrow and fear, I called out to the One who never left me, "You are enough for me. *Please* be enough for me."

With every fearful prayer, with every night that I wept and rocked a baby to sleep, with every morning that my broken body fought with pain, God taught me a new song. He was enough for me in every moment of pain, for *He* is the source of hope—not the tantalizing quest for relief. If He is the source of our joy, then we can never truly be without it. He does not ebb and flow with life's unpredictable surge of trials. His is a deep, deep well of joy that will never run dry.

## A Psalmic Pattern

Eighteen months in the psalms changed the way that I viewed suffering. You can't spend that long in the Bible's big book of poetry and not be affected by the habits of the psalmists. After a while, their thought patterns wrap themselves around yours. You begin to think like the psalmists, and that's a good thing. The psalmists were certain that God was with them in their suffering, and we have that certainty, too, when we read their words in light of Immanuel—*God with us*. I want to share this pattern of the lament psalms with you so you will know what to do when life sends you straight to the psalms for relief. We might think we are there to lament our circumstances, but that's only the first step.

Lamentation isn't a practice we are all familiar with, but the Scriptures teach us how to acknowledge our anguish before God. I found validation for my grief, confusion, and fear in the psalms. Many of the sacred songs of David begin with lament: his enemies want him dead and his life is falling apart. His desperation is nearly palpable. A couple of the psalms end on a bleak note—there is no resolution, only lament. I've felt the grief of those inconsolable songs when there doesn't seem to be a plausible, hopeful ending.

However, those psalms demonstrate that there's a comfort found in the act of lamentation. When we acknowledge our powerlessness to change our situation, we're also yielding ourselves to God's authority over it all. When we have a tight grip on God's sovereignty, this line of thinking seems logical. We believe that God can intervene, and we struggle to understand why He won't. And I think that, in that context, it is right to lament. We acknowledge that God is sovereign and able—and so even when He does not seem to be acting on our behalf, we must humble ourselves and cry out to Him. Who else is there to call on? There is only Him.

As I studied the Psalms in a position of lament and uncertainty, I realized that the unreconciled psalms of lament were the exceptions rather than the rules. Most of the psalms move through lament and grief and toward hope because of one significant shift: a meditation on God's character. When the writer remembers who God is and how He has been faithful to His people in the past, he ends by resolving to believe in God's continued faithfulness. This resolution usually comes after the pattern of lament, panic, and remembering.

Psalm 77 is a good example of this, so we'll follow it to illustrate all the steps of the psalmic pattern. Asaph is the author of this particular psalm. He was a gifted musician and poet who wrote Psalms 50 and 73–83. The layout of the 77th psalm is structured in a way that allows for grief but prods the hopeless toward the Hope of Israel. It doesn't leave us to live in our grief forever. But don't miss the fact that lament is its first expression:

> I cry aloud to God,
> aloud to God, and He will hear me.

*Lament*

> I sought the Lord in my day of trouble.
> My hands were continually lifted up
> all night long;
> I refused to be comforted.
> I think of God; I groan;
> I meditate; my spirit becomes weak. (vv. 1–3)

When I roamed my house in the night, in too much pain to sleep, I understood Asaph's ruminations. When I wondered about the future of the baby in our care, fear kept me from comfort. When I was afraid of who I might be on the other side of my suffering, I thought of God and groaned. I didn't understand how my life could be crumbling in so many corners. Asaph gives us the language of lament.

As we move further through Psalm 77, Asaph's grief turns into a panicked list of questions. He thinks back on the glories of the past and wonders if his life will ever be the same.

*fear*

*panic*

> Will the Lord reject forever
> and never again show favor?
> Has His faithful love ceased forever?
> Is His promise at an end for all generations?
> Has God forgotten to be gracious?
> Has He in anger withheld His compassion? (vv. 7–9)

The questions reach a crescendo when Asaph fears that the Lord might not ever answer his prayers. Have you done the same? Scrambling to put the shards of our shattered hopes back together, we ask (or demand), "Lord, why won't You fix this situation? Have You forgotten how to be good to us? Do you keep Your promises anymore?" Asaph said, "I am grieved that the right hand of the Most High has changed" (v. 10).

But it can't end there—and thankfully it doesn't.

The very next words of Psalm 77 say this, "I will remember the LORD's works; yes, I will remember Your ancient wonders. I will reflect on all You have done" (vv. 11–12). Asaph reflects on the history of Yahweh: how He redeemed His people, how the very earth obeyed His commands. You see Asaph's resolve strengthen:

> God, Your way is holy.
> What god is great like God?
> You are the God who works wonders;
> You revealed Your strength among the peoples.
> With power You redeemed Your people,
> the descendants of Jacob and Joseph. (vv. 13–15)

*Remembering*

Asaph pushes back against forgetfulness—against the temptation man has faced since the garden and the snake and the splatter of forbidden fruit on guilty hands. The goal is to remember who God is. It's the cure for the ache, for the suffering, for the longing to right what's wrong. The answer is found in the character of God. Asaph mentions two specific names from God's work of redemption: Jacob and Joseph—men who knew the Lord's presence up close and who could say, "He has been with me everywhere I have gone" and "The LORD was with [me] and extended every kindness to [me]" (Gen. 35:3; 39:21).

Remembering God's faithfulness is the turning point of Psalm 77, and from there Asaph moves to resolution. The perseverance of God's people in the past was born from His very present presence. Remembering His past faithful love is what helps us resolve to believe that God will not abandon us in our suffering. Remembering His steadfast love makes us certain that the answer to "How long, O Lord?" is always "I Am." Yahweh's name, called out from His own lips back in Exodus at the burning bush, is the way we persevere through suffering. *I Am* is how we hold on. *I Am* is with us. *I Am* is the one who sent Immanuel. *I Am* is the one

153

who sent the Spirit. *I Am* is the one who moves us from lament to hope.

He is the one who sits with us in our grief and lifts our chins, who pulls perseverance from our broken hearts. And it is *I Am* to whom Asaph turns in his lament in order to reset his mind. To believe in God's future faithfulness, we must look back at the past faithfulness of the great, unchanging God who has been with His people in their lamentations. Then, we can resolve to move forward with faith in His continued presence, no matter the outcome of our circumstances.

Lamentation, panic, remembrance, resolve. Let the Psalms help to anchor your heart in God's faithfulness.

### Faithful Love

Camping out in the poetry of the Bible was life-giving medicine during my weary months of waiting. No matter what fear cropped up in my heart, the Lord had encircled my heart and reminded me of His presence through His Word. As David wrote in Psalm 139, the Lord knew my every thought and held on to me with His right hand. I couldn't have escaped His comforting presence if I'd wanted to. (Not that I ever wanted to!)

Each day, I did my best to manage my physical pain, pour my love on both of the children in my home, and then lie down at night knowing that I could offer nothing to the Lord but my helplessness. He walked the floors with me, saw the midnight feedings with the baby I so desperately loved, witnessed my daily struggle to believe that He was enough for me if it all fell apart. Our attorney wasn't as optimistic as I would have liked; the depositions were messy; more than one of our long road trips were completely unnecessary and fruitless.

Every email, phone call, and piece of litigation brought different news. I was unable to depend on any human for security regarding our son's future in our family—but, to be honest, I needed the rug of illusionary security pulled from beneath me. I needed to lean heavily *only* on Christ. This was the place—the land of shredded control—where I would learn what Asaph meant when he said,

> Who do I have in heaven but You?
> And I desire nothing on earth but You.
> My flesh and my heart my fail,
> but God is the strength of my heart,
> my portion forever. (Ps. 73:25–26)

*[handwritten margin note: hope / resolve]*

I could lose my son, had lost my health, had lost what I thought was any chance of a healthy relationship with the church—but, tremulously, my lips echoed the sentiments of the Psalms. Essentially, it's this: *I am losing everything. But You are with me. So I have everything I need.*

I adopted the pattern of the psalmists. I lamented but remembered the promise of the presence of God. I drank deeply of His goodness in the Word. I didn't do this because I had arrived at some finish line of religious accomplishment. I was struggling mightily. No, I did it because there was no other place to go. The Lord was stripping me of my every confidence.

*Where else can I go?* There is only one answer, only one place to go—and it is always to the God who never leaves or forsakes. It is to the One who keeps every tear and carries every sorrow. I buried my face in the Scriptures because I couldn't do anything else. What the Lord taught me through the Psalms was that His faithful love most often looks like presence. The Psalms praise Him for His covenantal love, and the way He most often expresses that love is through His proximity to His people.

The language that's used to describe God's faithful love in the Psalms is often bookended with declarations that the psalmist will draw near and take refuge in Him. Take Psalm 36 for example:

> Lord, Your faithful love reaches to heaven,
> Your faithfulness to the clouds.
> Your righteousness is like the highest mountains;
> Your judgments, like the deepest sea.
>
> . . . . . . . . . . . . . . . . . . . . . . .
>
> God, Your faithful love is so valuable
> that people take refuge in the shadow of Your wings. (vv. 5–7)

Or even more plainly spoken is Psalm 73:28: "But as for me, God's presence is my good. I have made the Lord GOD my refuge, so I can tell about all You do."

These verses imply that God is always near. *We* are the ones who must draw up a chair. We convince ourselves that He is far away, but we are the ones who are refusing to listen to His voice or enjoy His nearness. Even when He seems quiet, He is constant. Jared C. Wilson says, "God is not only *not* giving you the silent treatment, he is practically *yelling*. The problem is not with his voice but with our ears. The more and harder we listen, however, the more of heaven's glorious music we will hear, and thus the more of heaven's glory we will see."[2] This is what living in the valley of the shadow revealed to me: He is near. I have only to drink deeply of His Word to know that He is with me.

When everything that matters to us seems to be slipping away, when we have to tamp down fear with the Word every day, when the outcome of our circumstances does not seem favorable, we can know without a shadow of doubt that God is with us in our suffering. In small, slow breaths, we can learn to say with the

---

2. Jared C. Wilson, *The Imperfect Disciple: Grace for People Who Can't Get Their Act Together* (Grand Rapids: Baker Books, 2017) 96–97.

psalmist, "It was good for me to be afflicted so that I could learn Your statutes" (Ps. 119:71).

## Discussion Questions

1. Does the idea of lamenting your griefs and fears before God feel natural to you, or does it feel like complaining? Is there a biblical precedence for lament?
2. In the psalms of lament, Glenna points out a pattern of lament, panic, remember, and resolve. Why is the "remember" step such an important part of biblical lamentation?
3. Share a time in your life when the psalms ministered to you with the language of lament and/or praise.
4. "I am losing everything. But You are with me. So I have everything I need." How can this be true when we have lost the dreams, hopes, or people who matter to us? Where must our contentment be anchored (see Heb. 6:19–20)?
5. In Psalm 139, David gives specific details about the ways that God's presence transcends geography, knowledge, and darkness. Pray through Psalm 139 and list some of the ways that God keeps His promise of being present.

# 10

# The Ministry of Presence

*The church—God's people—indwelled and sealed by
the Holy Spirit himself is an incomprehensible, spiritual-
literal reality. It is a prophetic hope that whispers of the end
when the dwelling place of God is forever among men.*

—GLORIA FURMAN

When my husband and I first moved to our small rural church,
I naively viewed ministry as an agreement between us and the
people we were serving. My husband would preach and provide
oversight, I would play the piano and teach children's Sunday
school, and the rest of the church would listen, follow, and serve
in all the other ways we needed in order to flourish together in
our community. I didn't really count on making emergency-room
visits, having impromptu marriage-counseling sessions, burying
church members, mediating between families, navigating infighting and power struggles, and trying to balance my own personal
trials with the trials of others. I didn't realize that ministry was
more of a verb than a noun and that the formula I had constructed was useless. When it comes to the way believers relate
to one another in the local church setting, ministry is not about

following a formula.[1] It's about the presence of God. And not just enjoying the presence of God but *practicing* it.

Think about it. Because every believer is given the gift of the Holy Spirit, every believer is the dwelling place of God. When we gather together to corporately worship, serve, give, observe the sacraments, and hear the Word, we are a group of people who are filled with the presence of God. I'm not saying that He's any more or less present in a particular number of people, but we are more *aware* of His presence when we recognize that He is present in the local group of believers who we worship with every week.

The New Testament writers give us a few metaphors for the church that explain who we are and how we should live. Followers of Jesus are called *coheirs* and members of the *family* of God, which communicates who we are in Christ. We're also called the *body* of Christ and a *building* that's constructed on the foundation of Christ, which illustrates how each individual believer contributes to the church as a whole. Additionally, the church is referred to as the bride of Christ—a name that expresses Christ's love for and commitment to us. Ministry flourishes when we know who we are and how we should work together for the glory of God.

In fellowshipping together, serving one another, and carrying one another's burdens, we experience the sweetness of the Lord's presence in other believers, and they in us. We each function out of obedience to the Lord through the strength and grace of the Holy Spirit. He isn't with us only when we're reading our Bibles and praying (though He isn't less present then, either). He is with us in all of life, and the obedience we display by loving and serving our fellow brothers and sisters stems from His presence in our lives.

1. I am not referring to church government or discipline, as there are clear steps and commands in Scripture for handling those issues. I'm referring to the way we obey the commands to love and serve one another. Our motives matter.

Through Him we live and move and have our being (see Acts 17:28). Through Him we exhibit His fruit and wear the demeanor of gentleness and grace that He values. We do not do these things apart from Him. And when we live and move and serve and love the family of God, we not only walk in obedience but also give one another the gift of God's nearness in our lives as He makes each of us more like Himself. Our enjoyment of God's presence is deepened when we see and relate to one another in the church with Him in mind.

## The Church Is God's Idea

God has never had to hatch a quick plan B. The church was always His idea. All the way back in Genesis 12, when He called a people out for Himself, He mentioned us—yes, you and me! He promised that through Abraham's seed, all the people of the earth would be blessed. And we were—we are, every believer—blessed by the atoning work of Christ at the cross.

Everything that Christ won at the cross has been given to us. We are called co-heirs with Jesus! Because of that work at the cross, God grafted into His family the non-Jewish followers of Christ. We are Abraham's children if we believe the gospel. This living body of believers in Christ, gathered throughout history and from around the globe, are His church. His idea. And if this is His idea, then we'd better get on board. When we know who we are in Christ, we can then minister to one another from the identity that we share in Him. God is our Father, and Jesus is our Brother (see Heb. 2:11). This makes us family—so we must strive to live as one.

Jesus talked about the church before His death and resurrection—specifically to Peter. The disciples' testimonies became the foundation for the body of Christ. Because of their message, the church grew and spread throughout the world. Everyone who follows Christ does so because Jesus's original followers spread His gospel. What's more, nothing on earth or beneath it will overpower the church or her good news. The church's continuing existence testifies to this truth. Human kingdoms have tried to bury the kingdom of God for centuries, but to no avail. No power on earth or in hell will thwart God's plans for His people.

We are not on our own here, though. God appointed Jesus as head of the church, as Paul explains to us in Ephesians 1:22–23. Jesus is often called the Bridegroom throughout the New Testament, and He promised to present the church as a pure and spotless bride before the Father (see Eph. 5:27). Jesus uses the example of marriage to communicate His devotion to His bride in order to help us to see how important the church is to Him. If He is committed to the church, then we should be too.

"But what about church dysfunction?" you might ask. What if you've been hurt by your church? Are we still tied to the church if we've had a horrible experience in it? I have asked those questions many times in my years as a pastor's wife. I've watched sin, fear, and suspicion shred our church family apart. I've been on the receiving end of church hurt, and I've inflicted a hefty dose of it as well. When we've been hurt within the church, it's tempting to settle for enjoying the Lord's presence from the safety of our living rooms. Yet God hasn't given up on the church. Neither should we.

Though we wreck relationships with our sinfulness and our messy, complicated lives, the church is one of the primary means God has given to us for enjoying His presence. We don't get to decide whether the church should be a part of our lives or not (see Hebrews 10:25). And if that statement makes you bristle with discomfort or reply with "Yeah, but . . ." then let's pause and remember where we came from before the Lord grafted us into one family.

## Brought Near Together

In order to commit to the body of Christ, we must remember who we used to be. We all used to be far from God. We lived outside the camp, so to speak—away from His presence. Our sin forged a gap that was too deep for us to bridge, leaving us unable to approach God. But our holy, just God is also our holy Justifier who bridged the gap Himself through His Son, Jesus Christ.

The church isn't some man-made, organizational attempt to keep all the sheep in a row. The church is God's gift to each of us who used to be far off but have been brought near by the blood of Christ. The church is the means by which we are sanctified, taught, encouraged, disciplined, and loved by God. Paul charged the body of Christ to minister to one another in these ways: "Warn those who are irresponsible, comfort the discouraged, help the weak, be patient with everyone" (1 Thess. 5:14).

The earliest believers depended heavily on one another—they cared for each other and reminded each other of what was true about Jesus. They lived in community, because their lives—both spiritual and physical—depended on it. Even today, the church offers protection for the wayward, comfort for the grieving, provision for the poor, and teaching for all. John repeatedly called believers to work out their obedience with love for one another, noting many times that they would be distinguished from the world by their love for each other (see John 13:35; 1 John 4:20–21; 5:1). We experience God's grace and nearness through His people, because the Spirit indwells them in the same way that He indwells you and me. Paul calls us a building that is "being built together for God's dwelling in the Spirit" (Eph. 2:22).

Though the Spirit of God lives in each of us individually, there is significance in the fact that He builds us *together* for His dwelling place. The New Testament writers used terms for the church that communicated a flourishing group that was made up of individuals with God-given gifts. In order for the church to function properly, we need all the members to participate. These terms in the New Testament are helpful because they illustrate the necessity of every individual. We are called a body with many parts, a building with many stones, a family with many heirs. It is Christ—the Head, the Cornerstone, and the Son, our Brother—who makes us one body, one building, one family where God is pleased to dwell. Though we hurt one another, we must look at each other with fierce forgiveness and a determined commitment to each other's good.

God did not call us together to live independently of one another. The building will crumble without all the stones, the body will die without all the organs, and the family will suffer without all the relatives. God can do anything He wants to accomplish His good purposes, but He chose to involve us in the process. After He brought us who were far off to be near together, He positioned us to need Him and one another, for His glory. This is a good thing, because it gives us the opportunity to enjoy His presence more.

When we understand that God is pleased to dwell in in other believers as He does in us, then we can see our way forward in the ministry of presence. It may be difficult, if you have a history of church hurt; but it is not impossible to set your heart toward loving the church and toward seeing her as a way to enjoy God's presence. If I believe that He is pleased to dwell in me, then I must believe that He is committed to dwelling in the church member who gets under my skin.

### Love What He Loves

During the final months of our second son's tumultuous adoption proceedings, I was given an official diagnosis of the pain that had crippled me for so long. Ankylosing Spondylitis is an autoimmune disease that, when untreated, fuses the vertebrae of the spine together in a permanent forward curve. It's a debilitating and painful disease that's difficult to diagnose and can cause lifelong, irreversible damage to the spine, hips, lungs, eyes, and heart, and to other peripheral joints. Unfortunately, it usually shows up with a couple of other autoimmune diseases tagging along.

A few months after my diagnosis and subsequent treatments, our son officially became our son in a small courthouse in Kansas. We were unprepared for the sudden end of such a difficult season, but we were beyond grateful. It was a sweet relief to talk about something other than illness and adoption and fear. I started sleeping through the night for the first time in six years, a gift that leaked down my cheeks in thankfulness the first time it happened. Winter was ebbing into spring, finally. We could laugh around the dinner table without the frayed edge of fear poking into our hearts. I had hope that the unsteadiness of the past year had leveled off.

The Lord had used His Word to seal up the cracks in the shaky faith I had in His goodness. I spent the early morning hours of each day enjoying His nearness, finding my satisfaction in Him, and learning to declare His sufficiency for my life. Yet I still withheld a portion of my heart from Him.

It was His church. That formula I had brought with me into ministry hadn't fixed anything. My husband and I had come to our church with a lot of naivete, and as we struggled to live in a dysfunctional spiritual family for the next decade, we had learned that nothing hurts quite like church hurt. Early on, I had lost any illusion that the church was a safe place for me, and during years of personal struggle, I had been afraid to share with my church how much I was hurting. If everything continued to be hard in ministry, would God's presence be enough to sustain me? Couldn't I just be happy in Jesus in the sanctuary of my living

room, where the sun rose through the back window and glim-
mered safely between the tulip trees? Couldn't I keep my arms-
length approach to church, for my own protection?

No. The answer is always no. To proclaim that the Lord is our
portion forever means that He is our portion in the places we are
most afraid to proclaim it. He can't be enough for us only in the
places where we feel safe. He has to be enough for us where we're
afraid for Him to be enough. He's not sufficient if he's sufficient
only when it's convenient. The Lord's sufficiency transcends fear.
He's enough for us when relationships are risky and when transparency invites criticism. He's enough when we choose to love
out of obedience to Him.

Jesus loves the church (see Eph. 5:25). Following Him
means loving what He loves. I could not claim to love Him while
divorcing my heart from the church that He loves. Being a part
of the body, the building, the family is a crucial part of growing
in godliness and persevering in the faith. We cannot expect to
disconnect from the church and still thrive. Even being present
in body but absent in love isn't enough. Sometimes you have to
resist your resistance and be *all in*, whether it feels safe or not.

### All In

When the Lord began to convict me of my emotional absence
from my church, we had just begun hosting a small group in our
home as a part of our church's effort to minister to one another
in smaller settings. I thought about how to do this in a way that
would proclaim that the Lord was enough for me no matter what.
Oddly enough, the answer was a five-pound package of frozen
ground beef.

I'd been reading Romans, and Paul's expression of "family
affection" in chapter 12 finally gave me a path to obedience. More
than that, it set me free.

Love must be without hypocrisy. Detest evil; cling to what is good. Show *family affection* to one another with brotherly love. Outdo one another in showing honor. Do not lack diligence; be fervent in spirit; serve the Lord. Rejoice in hope; be patient in affliction; be persistent in prayer. Share with the saints in their needs; pursue hospitality. (vv. 9–13)

"What if we feed people so that they'll be sure to come to small group?" I asked my husband after our first few weeks of hosting the group. "You know—'If we feed them, they will come'?" We couldn't really afford to feed sixteen people every Wednesday night, but if we found a way, maybe they would open up and talk to us. And if they talked to us, maybe we would learn to trust one another again. If putting a plate of spaghetti in their hands would help us to trust one another, maybe we just needed to make the spaghetti.

It wasn't complicated, but buying that first package of frozen ground beef invited risk into the safety of my home. It meant tearing down the walls that protected us from them—and setting fire to the very phrase *us and them.* There could be only *us.* One body, one building, one family.

For nearly a year, we opened our home every Wednesday night to a varying number of people for spaghetti, tacos, baked potatoes—whatever I could cheaply prepare for a large group. Every week we talked, prayed, laughed, argued . . . and, very slowly, we healed. Somehow, we healed. The presence of God was in my dining room, spilling out of the hearts of each believer who sat around my grubby dining room table. We were coheirs, each of us. Family. The same Spirit who urged us to open our front door was also urging the group to walk through the door and accept a plate of spaghetti.

The Wednesday-night family dinners became dear to me, with their paper plates, open-handed vulnerability, and chaotic clean-up. But they weren't the only day of the week that required me to resist my resistance to being all in. For all of the sweetness of those Wednesdays, I still dreaded Sundays the most. The walk from the church parking lot to the front door each week made me nauseated over the old feelings of betrayal I felt. But the folks who warmed the pews with me had endured the worst of the troubles with us, and we needed to learn to trust one another again—to worship the Lord together again in both spirit and truth.

Loving my spiritual family meant ordering my life around obedience. It would never happen accidentally. Jared Wilson says, "We treat the church the way we hope Jesus never treats us, keeping us at arms' length because we're weird or messy or socially awkward. But if the holy God of the universe affectionately welcomes all those losers to himself, who do we think we are when we refuse to do so ourselves? Paul says, 'Welcome one another as Christ has welcomed you' (Rom. 15:7). But until we engage fully in the messy community of discipleship, we cannot expect to feel Christ fully engaged in the mess of us."[2]

What I did to order my life around loving my church wasn't rocket science. It's simple stuff, really. Being fully present within my church may have felt like a complicated matter, but the steps of deconstructing the emotional wall I had built weren't.

I began by thinking about Sunday on Saturday. I made preparations for Sunday's lunch, laid out everyone's clothing, pulled out my sheet music for the following morning's service. I packed the diaper bag, stacked Bibles and notebooks, and planned an easy breakfast for the kids. Whatever I could do to ensure a smooth transition from the safety of home to the vulnerability of church, that's what I did. I made the decision on Saturday to be fully present on Sunday. And when Sunday rolled around, I looked people

2. Jared C. Wilson, *The Imperfect Disciple: Grace for People Who Can't Get Their Act Together* (Grand Rapids: Baker Books, 2017), 129.

in the eye and was honest about how hard my week had been instead of talking about the weather. My husband and I became determined to eliminate space between ourselves and our church members. Was it uncomfortable at first? Absolutely. Was it worth it? Absolutely.

The most helpful practice I adopted during that season was to take walks on Saturday afternoons and pray through the church membership roll. I prayed for every square inch of my local body of Christ. I picked apart the limbs and organs and prayed for individuals who got under my skin, while also confessing my own sins of cynicism and grudge-holding. I pleaded for the Lord to stitch us back together in love and prayed that He would have mercy on the whole wretched, beautiful thing.

Because she *is* beautiful. The church is the bride of Christ, and He loves her fiercely. Sometimes she is wretched. Sometimes I contribute to her wretchedness in the ugliest of ways. But she is His idea—His love—the object of His affections and promises for redemption. And this means that, no matter what, I must labor to love her . . . even—and especially when—she has hurt me. The truth is that I hurt her too. And yet here she is every Sunday, sharing a pew and a song and a communion cup.

The practices of opening my home, preparing my heart, and resisting my resistance were tools that God used to heal my relationship with the church. And because He is committed to keeping me humble and teaching me to treasure Him the most, He did this within the very same walls where my heart had been shattered.

If you've been hurt or ostracized by the church and you want to give up on the whole idea, you're not alone. Church hurt *hurts*. But Jesus loves His church, and He won't give up on her. Neither should we. I am certain that the Lord will honor your prayers for restoration, healing, and renewed commitment. Resist your resistance to being physically and emotionally present. Trust that the Lord is enough for you to be *all in*.

## There Is No Formula for the Ministry of Presence

There is no perfect church. Charles Spurgeon famously said, "If I had never joined a church till I had found one that was perfect, I should never have joined one at all. And the moment I did join it, if I had found one, I should have spoiled it, for it would not have been a perfect church after I had become a member of it."[3] Each local body of believers is made up of imperfect people who are slogging their way toward holiness. It should not surprise us when we hurt one another. Paul's letters to the early churches overflowed with corrections for fighting and exhortations for them to love one another. Peter's letters spill over with the same kinds of encouragements and rebukes.

The New Testament epistles are ripe with warnings about factions and infighting and strong with urges for the believers to love one another deeply. The backbones of these letters are reminders to us of our former identity as those who were far from God and our current identity as coheirs who are being built together into one building, one body, one family through the same Spirit who lives in each of us. We must fight for that intense love that covers all the ways we have failed one another.

For years I followed my old formulaic equation for ministry. We, the pastor and family, serve and teach *you*, the people, how to live. In return, *you*, the people, serve *us* by following like good little sheep. We'll all get along if we follow the formula. But that's not realistic—and it's not exactly biblical, either. What the Lord taught me on the Wednesday nights of spaghetti and slow-growing vulnerability, and on the Sundays of determined transparency, was that ministry was less of a formula and more of a practice of presence. Proximity was the way forward.

3. Charles Haddon Spurgeon, "The Best Donation" (sermon, Metropolitan Tabernacle, London, April 5, 1891).

Throughout redemptive history, the Lord has expressed His faithful love to His people through His presence. It follows that the way for His people to maintain an intense love for one another is through the ministry of presence as well.

Progress toward finding contentment in the presence and person of God began to take shape in my life with my church community when I ditched the formula and practiced proximity. I prayed for ways that I could declare God's sufficiency in my life and reject the fruit of discontent that had long fed my anorexic soul. If His nearness was enough for me, then I could safely expose myself to risk in my faith community—because my security was bound up in the faithfulness of God, not in the people of my church.

I stopped praying for my church to love me back and began praying that they would love Jesus the most. It is unfair to hang our contentment on the people with whom we worship and serve; they were never meant to be the anchor for our hope. Only Christ can shoulder the weight of our souls' satisfaction. Pinning our hearts' desires on Him frees the people of God from undue expectations. We can simply be a family who use our gifts to encourage one another rather than depending on one another for complete contentment. When we stop expecting our brothers and sisters to answer an ache that only God can answer, we can rightly see them as brothers and sisters, coheirs, living stones, and fellow homes where God is pleased to dwell.

It took time (and it's still taking time), but I'm learning that what my fellow coheirs need from me is presence. Just presence, *full stop*. Just knowledge that they're not alone in whatever dark valley they're walking through. As the Lord has done for me for years upon years, I need to sit near those who are hurting and extend grace.

I do it sloppily. Practicing presence reveals the selfishness in me, and I swallow a lot of platitudes in moments of awkward silence. Mostly, though, people just want you to be near them when they're suffering. That is sometimes easy and sometimes hard—and always needful.

What we need from each other isn't a formula for ministry or a churchy platitude. What we need from each other is presence. We need a coheir, a family member, a fellow living stone to help us find our anchor—to help us remember the words to the song we sing every Sunday, when we gather together as one family and declare to the One who unites us with His presence: "You are enough for us."

## Behold Your Future

Jesus said,

> I am the true vine, and My Father is the vineyard keeper. Every branch in Me that does not produce fruit He removes, and He prunes every branch that produces fruit so that it will produce more fruit. . . . Remain in Me, and I in you. Just as a branch is unable to produce fruit by itself unless it remains on the vine, so neither can you unless you remain in Me. (John 15:1–2, 4)

In my years as a pastor's wife, I have seen people both within and without the church blame their lack of attachment to the body of Christ on the other members in it. I've watched people wither up and die, unattached to the Vine, because they can't bear to be associated with any of the other branches. I've come close to withering up and walking away from the whole idea myself! And yet I cannot ignore the way that God persistently keeps His word to His persistently unfaithful people throughout all of Scripture. If He is committed to His people, then we must be too.

If we find ourselves constantly at odds with the people of God and church-hopping in order to escape hurts and grudges, then perhaps the problem isn't the other people of God as much as it's our own attitude toward them. Let's remember our coheir status: one body, one building, one family. It is likely that, though we have been hurt by other branches, we have also inflicted our fair share of pain.

Grace and forgiveness can flow through the branches when we recognize that without the grace and forgiveness of the Vineyard Keeper for our own lifeless limbs, we would not be able to extend or receive what we need from one another. Recognizing our common, desperate need for God's nearness keeps us attached to the Vine and to one another.

A few years ago, I went back through my journals from the periods of our most intense and painful days of ministry. Compelled by the Spirit, I blacked out every incriminating name. Love keeps no record of wrongs. The apostle Paul is clear in his instructions to this body, this building, this family that love requires a choice to forget the specifics.

Though my memory works better than I wish it did in this regard, time has blurred the edges of offense, and there are days when I have trouble recalling exactly what downed the ship. This is God's grace, and it is evidence that His commitment to His church is stronger than my commitment to my past hurts. He will see her through her sanctification. We can either walk in obedience and learn to love His vision for His bride, or we can characterize ourselves by self-victimization and find ourselves on the opposing side of God's plan to be with His people.

These branches that we're so beautifully and messily tangled up with? They're the fellow citizens of our future, better country. Let today be the day you behold your future and love the church by being with her.

## Discussion Questions

*Annette*

1. Have you experienced church hurt? How has it impacted your relationship with the church?

*Jenny* 2. Why is it not an option to give up on the idea of church, even if we have been hurt?

*Dorcas* 3. The New Testament writers use several different terms for the church: *body, family, building, bride.* What is the significance of these terms, and how do they communicate who we are and how we are to live?

*Sailly* 4. Share your thoughts on the ministry of presence. How do we enjoy the presence of God through the body of Christ?

*Jane* 5. If you are struggling to be physically or emotionally present with your local church, what are some steps you could take to be *all in*?

# 11

# Free from Longing
# and Face-to-Face

*Look! God's dwelling is with humanity, and He will*
*live with them. They will be His people, and God*
*Himself will be with them and be their God.*

—Revelation 21:3

My life isn't tied up with a neat bow of healing and reconciliation—and, likely, neither is yours. Physical pain still sometimes
crowds out my memories of God's faithfulness. I still harbor tiny,
ridiculous hopes that one day God will do something miraculous with my empty womb. I still fight every week to recognize
the coheir status of my brothers and sisters in Christ. I write this
final chapter knowing that, before I'm ready, I'll be lying faceup
on a cold steel operating table again because of one of the
diseases I will carry to my grave. I will think about Eve and the
snake and the fruit and will be tempted again to sing my song of
discontent.

But God is using the longings of my heart to teach me where
to go for true contentment. Every time there's an ache I can't fix, I
can look at the things that I lack and know that what I need most

is not healing or gifts that I can hold with my hands. Suffering has taught me that what we think will make us happy can be found and lost in a moment—but the promise of God's presence is a constant gift that we'll never lose.

Sometimes it takes cycles of trials for us to keep our gaze fixed on the One whom we long for. In this way, suffering is an unasked-for gift. Though I desire to move away from the broken years of my life, I want what I learned about God in them to accompany me down the path of sanctification. Instead of fearing what's next, I want to look for His presence the next time sorrow knocks at my door. Suffering is one way that God refines our faith and keeps us reliant on Him (see 1 Peter 1:6–7).

In Philippians 3, the apostle Paul encourages us to let go of whatever is behind us in order to press forward toward knowing Christ perfectly and one day being perfect in Him. Though he had suffered much for Christ and had grown in His likeness, Paul still saw himself deep in the process of sanctification. Every mile of our heavenward path is paved with both joys and trials. We won't reach full maturity in Christ while sojourning on earth, but we'll grow more like Him with each crooked step we take as we learn to sing of His sufficiency—both to Him and to the people around us.

Sanctification keeps us singing that song in whatever season we find ourselves. Our sorrows won't last forever. We can believe that He is enough for us now, because we know that He will be enough for us for eternity. It's that kingdom perspective—the *already/not-yet* posture of perseverance. The kingdom has come, but it is also still coming. God is with us, but He will be with us fully yet to come.

We Christians like to remind ourselves that we're not home yet—and though that statement conjures up in my mind thoughts of sticky summer evenings marked by mosquitoes and revival meetings in the little Baptist churches of my southern childhood, it isn't wrong. We're *not* home yet. I used to cringe when I heard that phrase, because I was afraid of both death *and* Christ's return when I was a child—whichever might come first. That quiet fear followed me through my teenage and college years and even into my adulthood. It wasn't so much the process of dying I was afraid of, or that I wouldn't be a part of the resurrected bride of Christ. No, it was less profound than that: I was afraid of what I would miss in my earthly life.

I thought I had a right to enjoy the common human experiences that we look forward to: marriage and intimacy, childbirth and parenting, growing in wisdom and milestones. I wanted to die peacefully at a ripe old age with no regrets and nothing to lose. When I had tasted all the goodness of earthly life, *then* I'd be ready for heaven. *Then* I'd be pleased to enjoy what God has to offer.

But that was before I knew the absence of children and the presence of sorrow and physical pain. Those old fears ruled my thoughts about eternity before I understood that my treasure wasn't actually any of the things that I hoped would satisfy my longings.

## Present Sufferings and Future Glory

In our past and present sufferings lies a glorious, forward-pointing arrow. You need not run after pain and suffering (the world is too broken for you to bother seeking them out), but they are gifts that graciously remind us of our temporary residence on earth. Interim conditions of pain or loneliness or fear cannot hope to match heaven's eternal absence of them.

Our final resting place will be free from the things that color our human existence. We will no longer hunger, thirst, or fight against the earth (see Rev. 7:16–17). God will tenderly wipe away our every tear, and our eternal existence will instead be marked by the *absence* of the things that plagued our lives on earth. In stark contrast to this fallen earth, where we scratch out our existence under the curse, we will be done altogether with *need* in our heavenly home. Heaven will be devoid of death, pain, grief, and crying (see Rev. 21:4).

We will no longer fight the urge to soothe the ache in our bones with inferior solutions, because we will stand, completely unhindered, in the presence of God. We will no longer hear the serpent's hiss and doubt that God is the answer to all of life's aching. Though we have struggled to sing confidently of His sufficiency when sorrow presses against our chests, one day we will sing of it in His very throne room before His very face. The only thing pressing against us then will be glory—only glory.

But until then, we slog forward, following the forward-pointing arrow that rises from either the memory of our pain or its continuing presence. Let your suffering serve you. Let it speak boldly of the *already/not-yet* status that you carry as an alien and stranger who longs for a better home, a better country, and a Savior who will "transform the body of our humble condition into the likeness of His glorious body, by the power that enables Him to subject everything to Himself" (Phil. 3:21). Because the truth is that these broken bodies are only temporary, and these sorrow-soaked days are a blip on the time line of eternity forward. We will be living in transformed, pain-free, tear-free bodies for a million years' time and will still have just *begun* to enjoy them.

There's hope in knowing that our lives here are small and short. We can fight for joy and cling to the sufficiency of God's nearness now because one day we'll sing next to His actual throne. We can persevere because this isn't all there is. If this tainted, post-Eden version of life were all we had, then we would be right to spend our sad existence devoted only to mourning our sufferings. We would be, as Paul put it, "pitied more than anyone" (1 Cor. 15:19). But the good news is that our troubles, though they are real and are cause for grief, are light and momentary compared to what's coming.

We can press on in perseverance, because God doesn't waste our pain. He redeems it to teach us that He is our treasure.

> Therefore we do not give up. Even though our outer person is being destroyed, our inner person is being renewed day by day. For our momentary light affliction is producing for us an absolutely incomparable eternal weight of glory. So we do not focus on what is seen, but on what is unseen. For what is seen is temporary, but what is unseen is eternal. (2 Cor. 4:16–18)

Do you see the hope woven into the apostle Paul's encouragement here? He doesn't deny that our bodies are wasting away. He doesn't tell us to pretend that they don't exist. Rather, he exhorts us to look with spiritual eyes at what is happening to us. *God is using your affliction to make you more like Him.* He redeems your pain by helping you to treasure Him more than any pleasure that earth could offer. The pain you feel now, though significant in its effect on your body or its tearing at your heart, is nothing compared to the eternal weight of glory that's coming. Your suffering, though profoundly real, is minuscule in comparison to the magnitude of the forever, everlasting, never-ending *paradise* ahead.

We are *not* home yet, thankfully. Though we may feel that sanctification is a wilderness we can't quit circling, the beauty of becoming like Christ is that it is forward-moving. Slowly, perhaps. With some steps backward, to be sure. But always moving forward and pressing on toward that eternal weight of glory. While we press through the story God has written for us, we can find comfort in the fact that He is with us in every moment of our sojourning. He will "personally restore, establish, strengthen, and support you after you have suffered a little" (1 Peter 5:10).

The God who called a people for Himself out from slavery in

Exodus, the God who preserved them through centuries of disobedience and broken attempts at holiness, the God who went to great lengths to live among His people, the God who became one of His people in order to save them, the God who raised Jesus from the dead, the God who has called you to salvation and to be His child . . . He is personally invested in your perseverance. He will be with you—He *is* with you. And one day He will raise from the ground your broken body, heavy with past remembered sorrows, and will transform it into something new that is perfectly suited to an eternity in the absence of pain, grief, sorrow, or death.

And the *absence* of things is only the beginning. Oh yes—absence is only part of it. Presence is the main event.

### Heaven's Tabernacle

I used to think that heaven might be boring—a lot of singing and bowing down and trying to figure out who had the more mundane existence: the angels or the humans. My lack of commitment to the Scriptures and my subsequent misunderstanding of them contributed to my perception of eternal monotony. But even in my churchy childhood, heaven wasn't painted as being much more than an ethereal existence of cloud-like happiness. That still sounds pretty boring to me.

The Bible doesn't give us all we want to know about our eternity with God, but it gives us all that we need to know. What we need to know is that eternity with God is eternity *with God*. Our perpetual future with Him won't be characterized by us but by *Him*. He is the gift of heaven. Pure, unfiltered access to God the Father is what our future will be about.

The thread that weaves together redemptive history is His commitment to being with His people. It began brightly in the garden but seemed to fall apart at the tree with the woman and the snake. We saw the Lord make a covenant to keep His word in spite of man's every attempt to fill his heart with the passing pleasures of earth instead of the enduring comfort of God's presence. Though they sought other gods, He kept His promise of presence through fire, cloud, and the tabernacle. The chosen, set-apart people of God tried to thwart His plans to be near them by demanding kings and kingdoms. He not only gave them kings but also lived among them in the temple Himself. They yearned for a deliverer when their refusal to submit to God's story resulted in their exile, but still He would keep His promises to them.

We follow the thread through the pages of Scripture until the Deliverer shows up in a manger in a stable. God's plan seemed to unravel at the cross, but that was the thread getting stitched so tightly that it would never lose its power. It was reconciliation and preparation and the tangible expression of God's promised presence. When we try to examine each individual thread in the story of God's presence among His people, it looks messy and tangled. But when we flip the tapestry and look at the other side, we can see the ways God has consistently kept to the path that He set on at the beginning.

In the desert long ago, there was a tabernacle—a place where Yahweh lived among His people. Israel followed Him all around the wilderness while they learned what it meant to be satisfied by Him alone. Their voices were rusty from slavery and exodus. They learned the song of satisfaction morning by morning, with each new sprinkling of manna, but struggled to understand its meaning. The tabernacle was a lead note that would point them to what He meant by being present with them in the temporary wilderness structure.

We should remember the tent and smoke when, much later, the apostle John would tell us that Jesus "took up residence among us" (John 1:14). God was keeping His promise to be with His people, as He did back in the dusty days of Exodus. He was sheltering His people in a tent in the wilderness, and He was sheltering

His people in the incarnation of Jesus. Jesus was *tabernacling*—dwelling among us—in order to be God with us. It's the same promise being kept over and over throughout Scripture.

We can keep following the thread because John uses similar language when he talks about heaven in Revelation 7:15: "The One seated on the throne will shelter them." God, who is seated on the throne of heaven, will shelter—will *tabernacle*—His people. He will pitch His tent of presence, so to speak, and it will fill all of heaven. The city of God will be full of His presence. That's the point. The whole city—not just a special, curtained-off area for the priests. Every believer will have pure, unadulterated access to His presence in every way, at all times.

Again, in Revelation 21, we find John using the same terminology: "Look! God's dwelling is with humanity, and He will live with them. They will be His people, and God Himself will be with them and be their God" (v. 3). God will live among His people. In heaven, though, His sheltering, His tabernacling, His living with us will look different from the earthly versions of His presence because sin will not permeate our understanding of His proximity to us. In fact, there will be no temple or sanctuary to help us understand His presence, because a structure will be unnecessary. "I did not see a sanctuary in [the city], because the Lord God the Almighty and the Lamb are its sanctuary" (Rev. 21:22).

Remember the temple curtain that ripped when Jesus died? In heaven the curtain is as noticeably absent as the temple structure is, because *God* is the sanctuary. He is the dwelling place—our dwelling place. He is the gift of heaven. His presence is the treasure. He is the song we will sing for eternity, because He will be our full satisfaction for the infinite days going forward. Our neediness will be obliterated in the face of His imminent, vibrant, eternity-filling *presence*. All the ways He pushed through our sinfulness and resistance were tastes—glimpses—shadows of the fullness of His presence we will enjoy in heaven. He is our inheritance. We will be free from any need or longing or yearning, because we will be free and face-to-face with the God we have yearned for since the day Adam fell.

## The Promise Is His Presence

Some days I yearn for what is to come, and some days I don't. The cares of earth clog my mind with work and worry and busyness, and sometimes I just *want* to want the glory that awaits us in Christ. The sorrow of suffering and deferred hopes truly is a gift when it unsettles us from mediocre wanting and uncovers the truth that our ache isn't just for healing and wholeness but for the One who can make us healed and whole.

For so many years I thought the answers to my prayers lay in the tangible good things that God could give me. But those things He has given me—children, physical healing, restoration—are grace *upon* grace. The bottom layer of grace that He's given me first is always Himself. Without Him, those other gifts would hold little meaning. His presence during all the broken years of my life is the first grace—the foundation that holds the other layers of grace upon grace upon grace. First it was Him. It was always Him. And it will always be Him. In heaven, it will be *fully Him.*

God's up-close, saturating presence will mean the absence of all the things that have clouded our minds with forgetfulness. We will never forget to sing of His sufficiency, because in heaven we will need no reminders. Heaven means no obstructions. We love Him now, though we cannot see Him—but then we will love Him fully, robustly, and unhindered because we will see Him as He is. I cannot imagine it, because I cannot imagine an existence in which I do not sin or yearn or hope for what I cannot yet see. But Scripture is clear. "I will give water as a gift to the thirsty from the spring of life. The victor will inherit these things, and I will be his God, and he will be My son" (Rev. 21:6–7). Pressing on in faith now, enjoying His presence today, is the taste we are given of what we can only try to imagine later.

Our inheritance, this unobstructed existence with God, is being kept for us while we are refined and protected by God until that day of reckoning. It's as sure as the cloud of smoke that filled the tabernacle in the desert. It's as certain as the baby's breath in the cattle stall, as real as the splitting of the temple curtain, as undeniable as the empty tomb and the resurrected body with the scarred hands and feet. It's as powerful as the rushing of the Spirit on the first Christians. It's as guaranteed as the dwelling of God in the heart of every broken-down, repentant sinner who falls forward at the foot of the cross and cries out, "You are enough to cover my sin!"

This coming day of the full, unobstructed, extravagant presence of God is as sure as the way that He walks now with every sojourner who sings of His sufficiency in the valley of the shadow. Though troubles may press hard on every side, His presence presses in harder, closer, nearer, deeper, truer. He is enough for us now, because He has always been enough. Garden, wilderness, kingdom, or exile, He has always been enough for His people. And when we wake up to our real life in the new kingdom, in the new city whose architect is God, He will be enough forever. He will be our satisfaction. He is every note—He is every crescendo and every rest. Every word to the song we will sing forever begins with His name and ends with His praise.

The promise has always been His presence. In every way that we need Him, He has kept His promise. He is enough. He will always be enough. He will keep every promise to be enough.

### He Is Enough for You

Maybe you're like me and you used to wonder what God's presence felt like or how you could be sure He was near. Perhaps you've wondered what you're supposed to do with the knowledge that He's with you. Maybe you've looked for Him in a quiet moment, a poignant sermon, or an emotional song. Maybe you've cried out in a crisis, "Jesus, be near!" and wondered whether He heard you at all.

You don't have to go looking for the presence of God the way that I do in that old, recurring dream I often have. You don't have to move the furniture in order to find Him or study the ambience of the church sanctuary for evidence of His presence. You don't have to pray an incantation or sing exactly the right song. You don't have to wonder whether He'll show up when you need Him to. His presence is not contingent on our invocation of it.

He has promised throughout all of Scripture that He will be with His people. We can trust that, since He has kept that promise for all of history, He will continue to keep it until we see Him face-to-face in heaven. If death couldn't hold Jesus in the ground, then no circumstance on earth will keep us from the nearness of God. He will never leave or forsake us.

And yet knowing, enjoying, and practicing His presence does depend in part on our obedience. The ways God has given us to do this are at our fingertips: He's given us His Word as the primary way to know Him, He's given us the Spirit to reside in us, and He's given us His church as a way for us to practice the ministry of presence. We have access to Him through Jesus's work at the cross!

When it comes to suffering, deferred hopes, or broken relationships, the answers that you need will always be found in Scripture. Turn to those reminders of God's faithful love for you. In both testaments, in each differing genre, in every book, in each story, on every page, in each chapter of God's Word is truth about God and how He loves His people. When we spend time knowing God in His enduring Word, we learn His character. We enjoy His presence when we spend time listening to His voice through the old and powerful words on the pages of our Bible.

Whether we're longing for healing, marriage, children, financial stability, friendships, purpose, or ministry, we should first align our desires with the truths of Scripture. It is not wrong to long for those things, but God's desires for us don't always look like ours. Though sometimes He is pleased to give us sweet gifts that we've prayed for, He is first and always concerned with the state of our hearts.

You might have every physical thing you could hope for and yet still find yourself yearning for satisfaction. Listen to that ache, and let it drive you to the Lord. Go to His Word and learn to love the One who satisfies our hearts and teaches us to hunger after Him. His desire is for you to know Him, to be changed by the power of the gospel, and to grow to spiritual maturity. His purposes for your life might include marriage, children, careers, health . . . or they may not. But as you enjoy His presence and learn His character through His Word, you'll learn to trust Him and His purpose for your life—whatever it looks like. His presence will be enough, no matter what.

When you're suffering or enduring loneliness, you're never alone. God dwells in you! "Don't you yourselves know that you are God's sanctuary and that the Spirit of God lives in you?" (1 Cor. 3:16). Whether you're walking the floors in fear and agonizing pain at night or facing month after month of crushed hopes, there will be no dark, shadowed valley that you walk by yourself. The Spirit is with you at all times. You can be comforted by the truths of Scripture, because the Spirit helps you to understand them. He can convict you of bitterness when someone else receives the answer to your prayer, and He can remind you that in Christ you have all that you need. His presence will be enough, no matter what.

You can both find and give the gift of God's presence within a local body of believers when you order your life around loving the church. Even a history of church hurt doesn't prohibit you from seeing the coheir status of your fellow believers. You can learn to be present during the sufferings of others, and you can receive comfort from the Spirit in others when you seek to be vulnerable and present. You can enjoy God's presence through His people even when it's messy or awkward. His presence will be enough, no matter what.

God will always be with us. Scripture is bursting with reasons for us to hold on to His promise of presence. I hope that whenever you pick up your Bible, you'll see the theme of His commitment to be with us running throughout the story of Scripture. And I hope you'll see that, because He is good, His presence is enough for us in every painful season and every open-ended wait. Our hope is never deferred in Him. We will always be with Him, and He will always be enough.

## Discussion Questions

1. Suffering is the gift we never ask for, but sometimes it is the one we need to help us fix our gaze on the Lord. How has God used a trial or a season of suffering to teach you about His character?
2. Heaven will be absent of suffering but filled with God's presence. Share some things you look forward to being free from when we are with God face-to-face. How might God use those things now to prepare you for eternity with Him later?
3. How has God used your afflictions to make you more like Him? Or how do you hope He will do this?
4. Think through the big story of the Bible and the ways God has kept His promise to be present with His people. How do the prophecies of Revelation 21:1–7 show that He will keep His promise of presence forever?
5. Where are you in life right now? Are you struggling to believe that God is enough for you? Are you holding fast

to His promises no matter what? Does your heart feel dull when it comes to what God says about His love for you? How does traveling the path of God's presence in Scripture encourage you to believe that He is with you now and always?